DIVINE MESSENGERS

THE NYENJOM OF HAA

Divine Messengers

*The Untold Story of Bhutan's
Female Shamans*

Stephanie Guyer-Stevens and
Françoise Pommaret

SHAMBHALA

Shambhala Publications, Inc.
2129 13th Street
Boulder, Colorado 80302
www.shambhala.com

Cover photo: Yannick Jooris
Cover art: Robert Beer

9 8 7 6 5 4 3 2 1

First Edition
Printed in the United States of America

♾ This edition is printed on acid-free paper that meets the
American National Standards Institute z39.48 Standard.
♲ This book is printed on 30% postconsumer recycled paper.
For more information please visit www.shambhala.com.

Shambhala Publications is distributed worldwide by
Penguin Random House, Inc., and its subsidiaries.

LIBRARY OF CONGRESS CATALOGING-IN-PUBLICATION DATA
Names: Guyer-Stevens, Stephanie, author. | Pommaret, Françoise, author.
Title: Divine messengers: the untold story of Bhutan's female shamans /
Stephanie Guyer-Stevens and Françoise Pommaret.
Description: First edition. | Boulder, Colorado: Shambhala, [2021] |
Includes bibliographical references.
Identifiers: LCCN 2020043750 | ISBN 9781611809183 (trade paperback)
Subjects: LCSH: Buddhism—Relations—Shamanism. | Shamanism—
Relations—Buddhism. | Women shamans—Bhutan. | Femininity—
Religious aspects—Buddhism.
Classification: LCC BQ4570.S5 G89 2021 | DDC 201/.44082095498—dc23
LC record available at https://lccn.loc.gov/2020043750

Contents

Part Three: A Delom Biography in Translation

FOREWORD BY KUNZANG CHODEN

Divine Messengers by Stephanie Guyer-Stevens with Françoise Pommaret comes at a most pertinent time, as a rapidly changing Bhutan is at a crucial juncture where we need to be reminded of our beliefs about the once vibrant and valid phenomenon of the *deloms*. The tradition of deloms, the women who return from the dead as messengers from hell, is quickly becoming yet another aspect of our forgotten history.

As I read *Divine Messengers*, I am reminded of my uncle who was a Buddhist monk reading to me when I was a teenager in the late 1960s. At the time I was studying in a Catholic convent in India. If my monk uncle were concerned that I would be influenced by the Christian faith, he never explicitly expressed his concerns, but he did try to infuse some Buddhist traditions into my life by reading Buddhist texts to me. He chose the stories of the deloms—or *delok*, as we referred to them in our language. My uncle read aloud but quietly in the traditional monotone-style of reading sacred texts, which often put me to sleep. But he never woke me up; he just continued to read. He believed that even though I was outwardly asleep, my deep subliminal mind was awake, and it had the capability to absorb the messages of the deloms who, too, experienced a form of deep sleep. That was how strongly rooted and vibrant the phenomenon of deloms was in our everyday culture.

Many years later, I was to hear the story of a real-life delom. A woman who worked for me lost her two-year-old son to a childhood disease. Some years after his death, when she heard about a delom in another district, she requested the delom for a divination to see where her son was reborn. For this she had to provide the age and the name of the dead child and the names and ages of the parents. The delom and the woman had never met and knew nothing about each other. The woman was really stunned when the delom sent her message saying that her dead son was reborn as a dog, but that if the mother conducted special prayers and raised a certain number of prayer flags, he would be reborn again as human being. The mother was shaken by this message because there was indeed a stray dog which had suddenly turned up at her door and refused to leave even though they tried to chase him away. The woman did not care for the dog at all and had even sent it away to another district with a migrating cattle herd. It was not only a two-day journey on foot to get to the new place but also required the crossing of one of the highest mountain passes (4, 109 meters high) in Central Bhutan. However, after a few days the dog had returned to her house and would not leave. The woman conducted the prayers, raised flags, and was kinder to the dog who stayed with her until its death.

This may sound like an extraordinary story, but such occurrences were mundane, everyday events in our past. We still lived in a world that held on to the magic and mystery of our natural and supernatural worlds. This world was kept alive to a large extent by those special people, the mediums, deloms, *pamo* (female) and *pawa* (male) *nyenjums, terdas,* and *jomos* who communicated between the humans and the spirit world and beyond (the hell realms in the case of deloms). It was not so long ago that we relied on these mediums to restore the peace and harmony between the humans and the spirits. The everyday sounds of the hand drum, the main instrument of the mediums, is slowly fading away and being replaced by the sounds emitted by our electronic gadgets. The people in my valley stubbornly and determinedly held on to the services of mediums for as long as they could. The last medium in my village, who was close to ninety years old and totally blind, used to be carried on the backs of people from village to village to perform rituals. She used to say that she was helpless because the spirits and divinities would not leave her body and that she had to submit to their command. This woman who could barely walk could dance tirelessly for hours while she was in a trance. She said that her body was possessed by the divinities, and that made the impossible possible. Like the deloms, who do not choose to become messengers, she was also chosen to serve as a divine messenger.

Recently I saw a message on a social media site, a plea with the photograph of a torn and worn-out handwritten text—the biography of one of the most well-known deloms, Karma Wangzin. The person who had posted the message was requesting that someone either rewrite or print the text that was in such a state of despair. The person considered it important enough to remember, honor, and perpetuate the story of deloms in our lives. In some ways it was heartening to see that although so much has changed and we have lost substantial facets of our traditional beliefs and practices, the phenomenon and relevance of deloms still appear significant and relevant and have made it to the digital age.

I would, therefore, like to commend the endeavor of Stephanie Guyer-Stevens and Françoise Pommaret on producing this book. The book attempts to document and analyze the place of extraordinary women in the Vajrayana Buddhist world. The authors are guided by the lives of the divine messengers of the past. This work is compelling, for it links the past with present day by looking at the ongoing practice of divine messengers in modern Bhutan. Their work will not only help sustain belief in this tradition but also provide a baseline for further research and documentation on Buddhist societal beliefs, attitudes, and practices and particularly for the study of the role of women in Buddhism.

PREFACE

We have written this book to bring to light a largely hidden phenomenon—that of women who are at once both shamans and Buddhist practitioners in Bhutan. We hope to also show that these divine messengers have found their voice alongside a male-centered religious establishment.

In doing so, there is no intention on our part of judging their legitimacy. We do not attempt to fit their stories into a linear, Western style of description nor to solve contradictions in their narratives.

In the course of our interviews with them, the women we met were positive about the prospect of having their religious work on behalf of their communities recognized and made better known. That said, we do not wish for them to become tourist attractions. While writing this book, we were in a quandary about how far to go in defining or naming the places where they live and how much we needed to leave intentionally vague. It felt like an ethical conundrum. The question became, do we publish a book or not? We decided to publish because of the value of their testimony. The light it sheds on this important and previously overlooked phenomenon is crucial to understanding the diversity of religious circumstances in our world as well as the important role played by women in the Buddhist Himalayas.

And so, for those of you who are so interested in the subject as to try to seek these women out yourselves, we first of all hope you do not and can instead find satisfaction in learning about them through reading this book. Sometimes the rare and precious things are best left alone. For those of you who do endeavor to approach these women, we hope you do so with sincerity, respect, and reverence.

This book is not an academic work but rather a testimony. It is the end of a long process that involves many people including several women of western Bhutan whom we interviewed. When we told these shamans of our intention to write this book, they expressed happiness that their roles in their society are being recognized. Our aim is not to present thorough academic research but to present the stories of the divine messengers in all their complexities. The Dzongkha terms used in this book are phoneticized as close as possible to the local pronunciation and are not transliterated.

We defined our collaboration in the creation of this book very simply. Stephanie would write the book in her own style while Françoise would be supervising and editing the testimonies of the women we interviewed. Françoise's interest in these women goes back to the mid-1980s when she did her PhD on the *delog*, or "women who come back from the netherworld." She feels honored to be given an opportunity to present the stories of these women to a readership beyond academic confines.

Stephanie Guyer-Stevens and Françoise Pommaret

Divine Messengers

Introduction

The ancient Tibetan name for Bhutan, the "Valleys of Medicinal Plants," only begins to describe the enormous diversity of life in the narrow valleys that wind around the massive mountains that define this extraordinary place on earth.

In any part of the world, life in the thick of wild nature is always imbued by the people who experience it with a free exchange between magic and reality, and Bhutan is no exception. Forms of the spirit world emerge from the sheer rock faces, the jungle, the vast expanses of high, clear blue sky, and the wind that blows through the tops of the snowy passes, whipping it all together. It was in this wild region, bounded by the steep Himalayas on three sides and by subtropical jungle to the south, where people first wandered over four thousand years ago. Like much of the Himalayan region, over the years it became a favorite refuge for those seeking to pursue their religious practice in solitude, and the practice of religion became entwined with the severely rugged country.

When Buddhism spread over the Himalayan passes from India, first to Tibet and then to Bhutan, it encountered a place where people took the spirits that inhabited the world around them as part and parcel of daily life. Demons and spirits were lurking behind every rock and bush when Padmasambhava, also referred to as Guru Rinpoche, first arrived there in the eighth century, bearing Buddhism. And although his intention was to spread Buddhism throughout the land, he did not destroy the various deities and spirits already present. Instead, working with the forces of the land and the sky to bring greater strength to Buddhism, he subdued them one by one, making each of them a servant of Buddhism, bound by oath.

Or so the story goes.

The result of this shift was that when people now acknowledged these spirits, they also acknowledged them as guardians of this new way of thinking and being in the world, of Buddhism. With the help of these spirits and demons, now transformed into deities, Buddhism spread throughout the Himalayas. And by adopting these deities, Buddhism itself changed once again into a new form known as Vajrayana Buddhism.

THE PATH OF INTERDEPENDENCE

Integrating the spirits and demons was not the only transformation that took place when the Vajrayana form of Buddhism evolved. Vajrayana Buddhism emphasized the concept of interdependence. Whatever you do to a tree or an insect or, in general, however you act in the world has an impact, a ripple effect that affects everything else.

You are always operating in the world in connection to everyone and everything around you. So two things emerged from that concept: First, you are completely responsible for how you operate in relationship to other beings, and second, and perhaps most profoundly, striving toward your own happiness and others' happiness is a necessary part of what is your gift of life in a human body. Your own well-being directly impacts the ability of those around you also to be happy in their lives.

There were other implications stemming from this way of being in the world. Because of this interconnectedness of all things in the universe, another important concept of Vajrayana Buddhism parallel to this view was that anyone could achieve enlightenment in one's current lifetime; it was not just something to be endlessly striving for and never reaching. It was in fact reachable. And likewise, it wasn't only available to the most dedicated ascetics; any yak herder or barley farmer could also achieve enlightenment.

This idea turned Buddhism on its head. Now, true devotion and practice could indeed lead a practitioner out of the cycle of rebirth, without even having to become a monk. That in turn led to the final interlocking piece of the Vajrayana system: in order to achieve enlightenment in this life, it was necessary to have a teacher who was schooled in the secret texts and rituals, someone who held the keys to unlock this path. The texts were voluminous, and the pathways forward many. Therefore, a spiritual teacher, a guru or lama who had the opportunity to study many secret texts and rituals, became a necessary guide to illuminate the path toward enlightenment. The many schools of Vajrayana Buddhism grew from the lineage of various masters who had gained that knowledge, passing it down through their teachings to their students who perpetuated it by establishing their own lineages of meditation practice, each creating a different migratory path, all converging in the same place of awakening.

Connecting with the Spirits of the Natural World

Let's backtrack a second here. Buddhism in its Vajrayana form was not considered to be a practice that was in isolation from the rest of the world. Rather, it was practiced in the midst of and on behalf of all sentient beings. One tenet of Vajrayana Buddhism is that the happiness of others is part and parcel with one's own happiness. There is no disconnect between personal and community happiness. In other words, there is no virtue found in misery; this practice was not about suffering hardships as evidence of enlightenment.

This idea did not begin or end with the human world, however. The principle of interconnectedness meant that each person was an integral part of the rest of the known world, and there was no way to escape that entanglement. In other words, everything that we do as humans is known to have an impact on everything else. The path to enlightenment came to have two parts: The first aspect was defined by the ability of a person to live in respect for all sentient beings. And second, by living in this way, a person would be finally delivered from the endless cycle of rebirth. The two were inextricable.

By integrating the indigenous spirits of the Himalayas and elevating them to the role of deities, Buddhism integrated the rest of the natural and spiritual world into this concept of a larger community, which acknowledged that we are all in this together, and we cannot disconnect our happiness as humans from the health and happiness of the world around us. Revering the spirits associated with nature, which were now local deities, in the end was an act of respecting humanity's interrelationship with nature.

It's here, at this juncture where we look out onto the world with human eyes and possess the idea of being entirely interconnected with everything we see, that the world around us can be understood as inhabited not only by the things we observe but also by that which we don't see. Spirits imbue every rock, stream, tree branch, bird, and gust of wind. It is also at this intersection of the human and the natural world where people for whom we use the blanket term *shaman* live. Nature is the larger assemblage of forces around us, and shamans are the ones who are able to tap directly into their power to impact us. These are the people who communicate with the spirits behind every rock and tree. They are the ones who translate for the rest of us how our lives are impacted by the spirits, or deities, and what they demand from us in turn. Shamans interpret the deities' concerns with the human world and translate those back to us, received in trances and related to us by means of rituals and divinations. This is still true in the Himalayas today, just as in all other parts of the world where shamanism exists.

This intersection of Buddhist ideas and shamanic practice became the local geography of Vajrayana as it gained a foothold in the Himalayas. With the arrival of Buddhism, religious pilgrims started traveling throughout Bhutan, as they did in neighboring Tibet, following the example of Padmasambhava, considered as he is to be the first religious pilgrim in Bhutan, or at least the first Buddhist propagator. He is revered in Bhutan as Guru Rinpoche, "the Precious Master," the bringer of Buddhism. He and the pilgrims that followed him were likely inspired by the wildness, which offered refuge in the rocks and trees and silence of the high mountains. The lived experience of being in the wild was part of and contributed to their Buddhist practice and devotion.

Put yourself in the shoes of people who know not only that every action impacts everything else in the world around them but also that they will have a life after this one. They know that what happens in their next life is up to them. With this knowledge, they have a huge sense of personal responsibility and also a great deal of personal choice. They know that if they do not behave according to certain norms, they will have to bear the consequences in this life or the next. They live enmeshed in the natural world and reckon with it daily—they are a part of the larger whole and view the world from that vantage point.

Where I Began This Journey

Now let me fast-forward many centuries and thousands of miles to where my own point of view started to form. As a child of two nature-loving parents growing up in North America in the 1960s and 1970s, my three siblings and I were expected to be outside as much as possible. During the summer we went outside in the morning and were not back inside until nighttime. As a little girl I never took off my swimsuit, even for bed, just in case there was a chance of taking another walk down the dirt lane to the beach. I remember going with my friend to the woods at the end of our street in the early spring, hoping to find lady's slipper orchids before anyone else did. I remember going to the meadow at the other end of the street in the heat of a summer afternoon, the sound of thousands of grasshoppers almost deafening; it felt so rich to have so many grasshoppers. I caught them easily and held them in the little cave I made for them in the palm of my hand, feeling the tickle of their tiny feet on my skin. Our childhood specialties were climbing granite boulders and trees, feeling the wind, stomping barefoot through mud puddles, feeling the currents of the ocean, and going to sleep under the stars, our dad pointing out the shapes of the constellations in the sky as we drifted off to sleep. Life was meant to be lived outside, according to our family. And that changes how you see things, how you relate to the world around you, when the things you know are things that are growing. Even if you live in a town, as we did, there is still huge nature all around you, and especially as a child that informs pretty much everything about how you see the world. That being said, we had warm houses, electric lights, soft beds to sleep in, and plenty of food in the refrigerator. We admired the wild, maybe, but we didn't really know what it was to have to live there.

Starting sometime in the late 1960s and early 1970s, some young people from the West who had traveled to what were then thought of as strange and remote parts of the world returned home to write about their experiences of shamanism; some claimed to have been initiated into shamanistic practices and offered to teach other people the ways of shamans. At that point many young people were "going back to the land" and looking for a return to some kind of spiritual tradition. Many people saw their connection to nature diminishing. They were genuinely searching for something to return them to a sense of having some kind of tribal roots. American society and culture were becoming increasingly homogenous. The notion of a shaman as someone who integrated magic and some kind of innate knowledge into a relationship with nature was just too intriguing. It was an ideal time to introduce shamanism to the West. Soon teachers of shamanism were plentiful in the 1970s Western world.

I remember thinking at the time that the idea of shamans as people who communicate with nature was really amazing. Shamans were, it seemed, a kind of magician who fell into trance and communicated with the spirit world, or who transformed into animals. They saw a larger picture of the human condition and in so doing helped to cure our ills. I was also brought up to believe that we had some kind of instinct within ourselves that modern culture had overrun. But the whole idea of people bringing to the West a concept that was birthed somewhere else seemed fishy, and the books that were being written about shamanism seemed to be founded on partially formed truths destined to enrich the authors at the expense of the people whose practices were being inaccurately described.

Needless to say, after a while I formed a pretty dim view of the Western literature on shamanism. I never really read these books much or pursued any study of it, because I assumed it was something locked inside others' cultures, perhaps for good reason; that was their thing to have and not mine.

But over time I was lucky enough to visit parts of the world where nature is still the driving force that determines all aspects of human life. In these places I have seen things that I cannot explain with my regular, daily Western mind. I've definitely seen firsthand that intersection of magic and nature. There is so much that exists in the world beyond human explanation of any kind, scientific or otherwise.

It's led me to conclude that interpreting natural forces is a kind of common sense, something that's not explainable in the regular day-to-day. But it is something that goes beyond simply careful observation of the world—that part of what happens when a human truly becomes more fully an integrated part of the world, and less of an individual. I've really grappled with trying to understand what magic is. That is such a wide term. Is it something that just happens? I don't think so. At least I don't think so anymore.

Reconsidering Shamanism

And that has brought me back around to reconsider shamanism and shamans: to try to figure out what it is, who they are, and to understand their world a little more deeply. I was helped along with this by a conversation with my friend, the Tibetan scholar Samten Karmay. Samten is not someone given to believing in magic. He is a serious academic, not given to raptures about spirit worlds. On the other hand, he has witnessed some things that stand outside his own capacity for rational explanation. As a young monk, he was present when the Dalai Lama was enthroned and carried through the streets of Lhasa on a palanquin. Oracles in masks and gorgeous costumes danced before him in trance. The oracles of the Dalai Lama have a critically important role as advisors. They are relied upon for predictions of all kinds. It was the oracles who predicted that the Chinese communists were trying to trick the Dalai Lama when they invited him to a play at the theater one spring evening in 1959. That was the night that the Dalai Lama, accompanied by his entourage, fled Lhasa and escaped across the Himalayas, eventually into India.

Those oracles Samten saw the day of the Dalai Lama's enthronement were not just people at the time, Samten explains matter-of-factly. They were people who had a spirit, a deity, enter into them, basically using their bodies as vessels for communication with human beings. The deities were acting through them as they walked ahead of the newly enthroned young monk, now the leader of the Tibetans.

Like others, Samten has wrestled with the question of what exactly is going on when things without any truly logical explanation happen. He points out as an example the fact that Mongolian shamans are again proliferating, even adapting to living in urban areas. This fundamentally changes the framework for how shamanism has often been explained. Since shamanism exists in almost every inhabited part of the world, Samten's conclusion is this: shamanism is a frame of mind. This frame of mind is available to certain people. It doesn't have a form of its own; instead, it adapts to what surrounds it—the geography, the environment, and the cultural conditions. As long as this frame of mind is accessible to people, shamanism will continue to exist.

I've come to the conclusion that looking at shamanism as a way of seeing the world is, in fact, possibly even necessary to understanding something very essential about our own humanness and to unlocking a big piece of the almost-forgotten story of ourselves as animals in the world, here among other beings.

MEETING FRANÇOISE POMMARET

Françoise Pommaret had a different experience during her childhood in the Congo. She was sheltered from the wild natural world around her—the huge Congo river, the savanna, and the deep equatorial forest. These natural elements were considered to be full of dangers and, in a way, full of untamed demons. She did not admire, did not know the wild and only learned to appreciate it once she came to the Himalayas.

However, in the Congo, she became aware of the world of witchcraft from a young age, knowing that intermediaries can act upon the unseen. When I first met Françoise in Thimphu, Bhutan, in 2011, she told me about the *delom* (also known as delog)—women who had died, traveled to the Tibetan Buddhist hells, and returned to live as advisors for their communities. She told me how the members of the community rely on these women to help them prepare for their own deaths by teaching them how to live a more spiritual life and by helping them atone for any sins they might have committed.

The deloms also help find out how their relatives are managing the postmortem state and whether they could do anything to help move them out of the hells, because after all, the hells are not called "hells" for nothing. The Tibetan hells as described by the deloms are the worst possible scenarios that you could possibly wrap your head around and then some. The hells are a huge concern for Bhutanese Buddhists, and the deloms are advisors with firsthand information about them, specifically how to avoid spending time there and how to live a better, more devout life while you still have your precious human body to reside in.

I didn't really understand it all when Françoise first explained it to me. She told me that she had met some of these deloms, but she thought that they might be diminishing in numbers. I was deeply intrigued and suggested we go out in search of the remaining deloms of Bhutan—to interview this vanishing group together before they disappear entirely. She readily agreed, and so we began.

Instead, we found these women in a whole variety of forms across the landscape of Bhutan, active players in people's daily lives.

For me, Françoise opened a door to the world she had begun to explore as a young graduate student decades before we met.

Françoise was doing graduate work in Paris and searching for a topic for her PhD in anthropology with a specialization in the Tibetan Himalayan world. She remembers: "One of my professors told me she knew of biographies of people who travel to hell and come back to give messages to the living. She suggested that I could study this collection of works from a historical perspective. Maybe I could even to do a translation."

After reading several biographies and various texts related to India, China, and Central Asia, she saw a pattern emerge. There was a whole genre of biographies about people who die, travel to the hells, and then return to life. She was already thinking about going to Bhutan, so she began to translate a biography from there. She was young and ready to go out into the world, and so in 1981 she headed to Nepal to see what she might learn there while she waited for her visa to Bhutan.

She was in the village of Boudhanath in Nepal when she met a young man from the Helambu region (Yolmo), a culturally Tibetan area north of Kathmandu. She mentioned to him something about deloms, and he told her casually that there was a delom in his village. "I was stunned, stupefied, whatever you want to call it," she recalls. "I had absolutely no idea or expectation at all that this was still real. Until that moment, for me, this was something entirely historical. And now, here was this young man telling me, as if it was the most common thing, 'Oh yeah, I know one of those deloms.' And he offered to take me to his village."

Françoise contacted her professor back in Paris to let her know. This was no longer a PhD based on textual research, she explained. "Go with it," was her professor's advice. This is how she was able to meet a living delom for the first time.

"When I first arrived in Bhutan, I started asking if anyone knew whether there were any deloms in Bhutan. Everyone I asked in western Bhutan said no, maybe because I was a newcomer or maybe because I did not know how to ask, but I kept asking. Finally, I asked friends from eastern Bhutan. 'Yes, there is a delom in our village; would you like to meet her?'" So, in 1982 Françoise went with friends to eastern Bhutan with a set of questions, a tape recorder, and a camera.

They traveled east in a jeep to the delom's village in Wamrong, an arduous three-day drive. The delom lived in a bamboo house on stilts, common in eastern Bhutan at that time. She was definitely not rich. While they were there, as it was an auspicious day in the Buddhist calendar, she had visitors over asking about their dead relatives. The delom, who had died and went to the hells guided by the deity of compassion, Avalokiteshvara, had returned with messages for the living from their deceased loved ones. Françoise duly recorded her. It was exactly the same pattern that she had read about in the historical delom biographies, except that according to those biographies, the deloms only traveled to the hells once, and this woman had gone many times. Now Françoise understood that she had a completely different direction to follow in her work.

The Wamrong delom mentioned to her the existence of another delom, a young woman who was said to be the reincarnation of the delom Karma Wangzin, in Khamdang, an area that borders to the northeast and east the frontiers of Arunachal Pradesh in India and Tibet in China.

The second delom lived in the village of Jangphu at an elevation of about 2,300 meters. When Françoise met her she was seated very straight, wearing a traditional dress called a *kira*, a maroon jacket, and a yellow scarf with religious symbols, holding a prayer wheel. In front of her there was a little table with flowers and incense sticks. She began to recount how she became a delom.

She was born into a poor farming family in September 1962. After her first "death," she was proclaimed a delom, and she then said, instructed by Avalokiteshvara, that her name was Karma Wangzin. The people of the region came to consult her to find out where their dead relatives were, which rituals would alleviate their sufferings, what was causing certain sicknesses, and generally to seek guidance on their problems. She did not go to births or funerals and she didn't travel because the world was full of impurities that could make her sick.

Françoise started to suspect that the tradition of the deloms might have something to do with shamanism. She still finds the term difficult to use because it is so loaded in the West. Shamanism has been called by Professor Hamayon, a specialist of shamanism, in French an *auberge espagnole*—you can put whatever you want in there, anything goes. However, Françoise decided it was the best description after all, using it in the same sense as the book *Dozing Shamans* does, which focuses on Eastern Nepal and is written by the anthropologist Philipp Sagant. She ended up referring to the deloms as shamans throughout her PhD dissertation.

OCCUPYING ANOTHER PLACE OF MIND

To talk about the women described in this book means we must distance ourselves from the strictly tangible world we live in and allow ourselves to occupy another place, one in which the wild of the natural world is a part of us and we are a part of it.

As our human society moves farther from a daily interconnection with wild nature, we precariously move farther from our selves, and as we do so, we risk misinterpreting and idealizing, or alternatively disregarding, the wisdom that arises from what is simply our natural habitat and the human responses we have to it. This relationship is full of magic—demons and deities, power and potency—always with the veil of death and life never far from one's consciousness.

And so, in this inquiry we have made an effort to understand the stories of these women who are shamans and Buddhists, who are still very relevant in modern Bhutan. Just to clarify here at the beginning, I am not a scholar of Buddhism or an initiated practitioner. I am a writer, a journalist, and a generally curious person who has met some people (particularly Françoise Pommaret and also Samten Karmay, Chencho Dorji, and numerous others) who have been kindly willing to answer my endless questions. Apart from that, pursuing an undergraduate degree in religion provided me with the simple skill of questioning how religion functions as part of a society, that is, how the fabric of religion is woven by the human society it responds to. This is not to reduce religion in its importance or to say that religion is simply a by-product of human life—I'm not entering into that debate. Rather, my personal goal is to understand its intrinsic and necessary role in the life of a human. Can religion sit comfortably at that intersection of being within and of the natural world, where shamanism exists? Through giving a voice to these divine messengers, I hope we can at least begin to better understand that question.

THE WHEEL OF LIFE MURAL AT TRONGSA DZONG

PART ONE

Those Who Return from Hell

I

What about That Word, *Shaman*?

In this book, Françoise and I do not question whether shamanic practices in Bhutan truly access different realms. Its manifestations are tangible and part of people's lives in Bhutan. We are not judging whether the shamans themselves are pretending to be shamans, whether they are actually in trance, whether their divinations are accurate, or whether they actually die and come back from the dead. The shamans, their patrons, and their communities have a real and viable relationship that is alive and well in modern Bhutan, and that's where we begin.

The lives of the active shaman women whom we had the good fortune to interview have afforded us a tiny glimpse into what we thought, at first, might be a vanishing culture. But it is in fact flourishing in modern-day Bhutan, adapting to the rapid growth of the human environment that is fast overtaking the once deeply quiet valleys of this most remote and beautiful Buddhist kingdom.

In order to place the stories of the women in this book within the framework of shamanism, we need to have a shared context for what shamanism means. As I said earlier, shamanism is difficult to define, but some explanations might be useful, especially in the context of Buddhist Bhutan. There are many people who are practicing Buddhists or students of Buddhism who have not been exposed to these shamanic traits. And so, it follows that there are many Buddhist practitioners and scholars who find the idea of connecting shamanism with Buddhism to be incongruous and not in keeping with "true" Buddhism. The problem is, definitions aside, dogma aside, purity aside, all those things aside, it is there, in practice, an intermingling of Buddhist and shamanic views and rituals. It's hoped that this simple explanation will be useful to piece together the logic of the shamanic practice within Vajrayana Buddhism and to understand why it is so inextricably a part of this form of Buddhist practice in the Himalayas.

Todd Gibson presents a shaman in this way: "If a person is recognized by his own society as being in direct contact with the divine or extrahuman, however society defines it, by virtue of concrete demonstrations of unusual or unique capabilities, then he or she is a shaman."[1]

Geoffrey Samuel defines shamanism as "the regulation and transformation of human life and human society through the use, or purported use, of altered states of consciousness by means of which specialist practitioners are held to communicate with a mode of reality alternative to, and more fundamental than, the world of ordinary experience."[2]

In other words, shamans are actually more like vehicles for deities who use a human to be able to express themselves to humans living in the earthly realm. Specific to Buddhist shamanism, Homayun Sidky says, "The powers of the dharmapālas, the pre-Buddhist deities that have been transformed into the protector of Buddhism by Padmasambhava, are considered to be more efficacious and immediate in the worldly affairs of humans because of the fact that the lower gods, so to say, are able to do what the transcendental deities usually do not, which is to communicate directly with supplicants through the vehicle of mediums."[3]

These Bhutanese shamans themselves don't have knowledge of the topics that the deities address through them. In fact, they are usually relatively uneducated and have little or no ability to even read. Yet in their trance state, they are sometimes even able to speak in Tibetan, the language that is primarily spoken in the monasteries. Thus, the shamans are "just the messengers" of the divine.

It would take some pretty broad strokes to talk about shamanism worldwide, and I don't have any qualifications to do that. But if we pin it down to the Himalayas, it's possible to see that there are some commonalities that occur throughout the region, and it's possible to make generalities about Himalayan shamans. Most of them go into a trance in some form. Likewise, most make a trip to the netherworld or hell realms. They share a strong fear of pollution, not just the environmental kind but also one that is incurred from exposure to impurities (negative thoughts, emotions, and karma) of others that ordinary people might not ever be able to detect. As a result, they all have special dietary requirements, and they usually have had some kind of initial disease, often a combination of psychological and physical ailments, which are understood to be indicators of having special capacities.

In Bhutanese languages there is no word for *shaman* as such. Instead, there are a series of specific terms that refer to people who have a shamanic experience. Pamo, pawo, and nyenjom are possessed by local deities, and then there are delom, rizam, and khandrom who are connected directly to the Buddhist deities. All of these types of shamans are what we call "divine messengers."

Because the practice doesn't seem traditionally Buddhist, and because in Bhutan it has roots in a set of non-Buddhist beliefs included under the umbrella of the Bon tradition, the Bhutanese realize it is not based in Buddhist practice. Nevertheless, they don't consider themselves to be non-Buddhist when they participate in shamanic rituals because both sets of beliefs are now so intertwined.

For the most part, witnessing these shamans is a quiet undramatic affair. Imagine a room in a wooden house set into the side of a steep, terraced hillside. The windows are open to the breeze, and you can hear the sound of someone chopping wood across the valley. Inside the room there is a low table set with a large bowl filled with sticks of incense chosen for its ability to purify the air and ether and protect from any negative influence brought by visitors. A small Bhutanese woman with short cropped hair, dressed in a traditional Bhutanese kira, a long dress pinned at the shoulders, is sitting on the floor. She might be starting to rock as she enters a trancelike state. It's a quiet afternoon; the sun is already behind the tall mountains beyond the hillside where the house is perched, and the cold, thin air runs through the dark green pines that rise above the rice fields. The elements are quiet outside, while the shaman we are here to meet struggles with a deep inner turmoil that is inescapable to her, that drives her to carry on this role, whether she has chosen it or not. This would be the typical scene that we encountered as we made our way to meet these divine messengers.

Likewise, there is nothing really exciting that happens to someone who is witnessing a Bhutanese shaman, except perhaps gaining some insight into the problems one had hoped to resolve by seeking the shaman's advice in the first place. There are no wild, hallucinogenic all-night trances. In fact, Bhutanese shamans never use hallucinogenics of any stripe. Any substance that could be altering the body and the mind of the practitioners is frowned upon, as they have to stay pure in order to connect with the divine realms. There is no need for an amplifier; she can hear them loud and clear.

The Difference between Oracles and Deloms

There are different types of divine messengers, and their type depends on their capacities. Oracles are transmitters of a deity, which helps them to answer questions about daily life. They are vessels which a deity possesses in order to convey a message. Their status is often more elevated due to their association with high lamas. The Tibetan state oracle predicted the fall of Tibet, for example, and also divined the route that the Dalai Lama needed to take to escape safely to India in 1959.

As the Dalai Lama has explained,

> The word "oracle" is itself highly misleading. It implies that there are people who possess oracular powers. This is wrong. In the Tibetan tradition there are merely certain men and women who act as mediums between the natural and spiritual realm, the name for them is *kuten*, which means literally the "physical basis."

He continues,

Also, I should point out that while it is usual for people to speak of oracles as if they were people, this is done for convenience. More accurately, they can be described as "spirits" which are associated with particular things, for example a statue, people, and places.[4]

Homayun Sidky explains the difference between shamans and oracles this way: "'Spirit adhesion' better describes what happens to the shaman than 'spirit possession,' which more aptly depicts the oracle, or *kuten*'s experiences."[5] *Kuten* translates directly as support of the body, which means a spirit or deity enters and uses the body as a support.

Deloms partially belong in the category defined as transmitters, but not entirely, since the Lord of the Dead doesn't speak directly through them. When a delom "falls dead" while someone consults her, she is not being possessed: she is returning to the hell realm and communicating with the Lord of the Dead. And when she "comes to," she is paraphrasing what the Lord of the Dead has told her. She has been a student, however unwillingly, of the Lord of the Dead in the hell realms and comes from that experience with the capability to be a teacher in her own right.

BUDDHISM AND SHAMANISM IN BHUTAN AND TIBET

I realize I'm going back and forth between Tibet and Bhutan, so I feel I should point out here that while Bhutan is distinct from Tibet, the two are connected culturally and religiously. In Bhutan there are nineteen languages, all of which, with the exception of Nepali, belong to the Tibeto-Burman linguistic family. The area often called cultural Tibet is today made up of several regions in China and is home to several languages, although when people speak broadly of Tibetan language, they usually refer to the language of central Tibet.

In Bhutan, the primary language is Dzongkha, the language of western Bhutan and the country's national language. Dzongkha and Tibetan both belong to two different subcategories of the Tibeto-Burman linguistic family, and they have enough differences in pronunciation, vocabulary, and grammar that the speakers of one can't really understand the other, like French and Italian.

However, the language called Classical Tibetan, used in monasteries, was for centuries the religious language of all Tibetan cultural areas, including Bhutan, Mongolia, and Ladakh in modern India. It was even used as the written language of Bhutan until 1971, when Dzongkha became a written language. Some of the religious words are common in the spoken languages of Tibet and Bhutan and are mutually understandable—Tibetan and Dzongkha share a written script. While Tibetans and Bhutanese can read each other's languages, they might not be able to fully understand the meaning. And just to clarify, the way that Tibetan words are sometimes written in Roman script bears little to no resemblance to the way that they are pronounced. In this book, the choice has been to transcribe such words phonetically for easy reading.

Another tether between Tibet and Bhutan is religion, since Vajrayana is considered a Tibetan Buddhist tradition. Vajrayana, which also spread to China and Japan, is known by other names as well: Esoteric Buddhism, Secret Mantra, Tantrayana, and the Diamond Path. In the Tibetan tradition, it breaks down in turn into different sects, the largest ones being the Nyingma, Sakya, Kagyu, and Gelug, which branch off in several subsects. In Bhutan the main sects are the Kagyu subsect known as Drukpa and the Nyingma. The Gelug, who had political authority over most of Tibet starting in 1642, has the Dalai Lama as its ruler. However, the Dalai Lama never held any significant influence in Bhutan.

To relate this all back to shamans in Bhutan, the shamanic practitioners discussed in this book consider themselves to be part of the Nyingma and Drukpa traditions, which are known for incorporating mysticism into their practice.

Bhutan strives to distinguish itself from Tibet to the outside world, pointing out that although it shares a language group and religion, it has never been part of political Tibet. In fact, Bhutan was created as a state by the Zhabdrung Ngawang Namgyel, who fled Tibet in 1616 because of a long-standing rivalry and an assassination attempt, but that story is for another time. The point is, Bhutan was partly created as a state in reaction to the Tibetan political dominance of the region in the seventeenth century. The Tibetans invaded Bhutan many times during this period. (The Bhutanese are quick to point out that the Tibetans were always defeated.)

Aside from these historical and cultural differences, there are commonalities in Buddhism as it is practiced in Tibet and in Bhutan. For centuries, Bhutanese practitioners went to Tibet to study with Tibetan masters, and Tibetan masters traveled to Bhutan to teach. Eventually, this exchange happened in reverse, with some Tibetans also seeking out Bhutanese as teachers.

Buddhism deals in the larger questions of life, death, and reincarnation, and as part of that, whether your life is a virtuous one and therefore whether you will travel to the hells after this life. Buddhism is deeply ingrained in the psyche of the Bhutanese, and, while looming large, is not necessarily a daily concern. Like people all over the world, the day-to-day concerns are the well-being of their family, their livelihood, their immediate surroundings, and impacts on them. Most Bhutanese focus on the local deities to help solve these concerns. As a shepherd once told Françoise, "The gods are part of our daily life. Buddha is for the afterlife."

It is at this juncture that the women interviewed for this book enter the picture. Although we imagined that we were searching out deloms, the arbiters of a very specific, extraordinary experience— women who die and travel to the hells, returning to life with specific messages for the living—in fact, what we found was that the term *delom* was stretching, adapting, and transforming through its interaction with a whole range of women with varying spiritual capacities, all of whom are divine messengers.

Variously called *nyenjom*, *pamo*, or *rizam*, these women become channels for the local deities. Whether they enter into a trance or not, they help people find answers, heal the sick, and appease the local deities who might have been disturbed by environmental or karmic imbalances. It's a delicate and tricky role. To a Buddhist shaman there are many sources of impurity, and their lives tend to be fraught with physical and mental illness due to their exposure to such imbalances. Many of the deities that speak through the shamans are local deities that have been transformed into protectors of Buddhism. The messengers of these deities are thus as Buddhist as they are shamanic, representing how these two strands are inextricably intertwined in Bhutanese society.

2

RETURNING FROM THE DEAD

I first traveled to Bhutan in January 2011 to document Queen Mother Ashi Sangay Choden Wangchuck's work to empower women generally and to eradicate domestic violence in the kingdom specifically. It was also on this trip that I first met Françoise. I was staying in Thimphu, the capital city of Bhutan, at the little Yeedzin Guest House, located behind an old stone wall and swinging iron gate near the center of town. The sun was already low on this cold early January day. It was my second evening in Thimphu. I was jet-lagged and still dealing with the altitude change, still trying to figure out where exactly I had landed. The sun was setting somewhere behind the hills and the mountains beyond them, when Françoise and I sat down for tea in the little guesthouse restaurant. The simple wooden walls were unadorned, and the wooden seats were covered in well-loved cushions with woven wool covers. It was too early for dinner, so we had the place mostly to ourselves as we drank our milk tea. At that point I knew next to nothing about the place where I was, so Françoise and I had plenty to talk about. I bombarded her with questions and she willingly obliged. We talked about life in Bhutan and about the role of women, since that was my lens into this place. Finally, I asked her about how she came to be here, and in the course of that first conversation she began to reveal to me the world of the deloms.

A delom, or *delog* in Tibetan, she began, is a woman who travels to the hells. They die, visit the hell realm, and when they return to life, bring messages to the living from Yama himself, the Lord of the Dead. The messages teach Buddhist practice, especially how to live a virtuous life in order to avoid ending up in the hells. Additionally, if you are concerned that one of your deceased relatives might be there, the messages also are about what you need to do, here in the land of the living, to help your relations be released from the hells sooner. Deloms are able to die many times during their lifetimes, each time bringing back new information, new messages and instructions from the Lord of the Dead for the living.

The delom practice is ancient. There are historical testimonials dating back to the twelfth century, and of all the divine messengers they are the most entrenched in Buddhism. Their messages generally do not have much to do with the local deities who guide daily life decisions for many of the villagers. Deloms focus on the larger picture: the stories of life and death, karma and retribution, reincarnation and the hell realms that await those who are not conscious of their actions during their lifetimes or those who are aware but haven't performed any acts of retributions for their past misdeeds. The deloms live in the larger world of Buddhism itself.

Françoise explained in a matter-of-fact way that, for this reason, deloms were and are indeed teachers; their knowledge has been gained from research in the field, so to speak, gained by dying and traveling to the hells with no less than the Lord of the Dead as their guide.

I was astonished. Mystified. I was in totally over my head, way beyond my ken. My knowledge of Tibetan Buddhism was zero to none. Maybe I had a vague idea of the purpose of a prayer flag based on what had been explained to me by someone who had hung them in their backyard in California. Now here I was in Bhutan, and this was not some faraway, magical thing. The deloms that Françoise was telling me about were simply part of human life here—raw, simple daily life—no adornments, no California backyard version of events. Since I happened to be there with my recording equipment, I offered to record an interview, and she agreed.

I returned to Bhutan in late March to complete the work I had gone there to do in the first place: to document a trek with Queen Mother Ashi Sangay. I returned to Thimphu and began to go through tape of the previous two weeks, sending files to one editor in the United States and another in the Netherlands, and spending a lot of time walking between my guesthouse room and the local internet café. Françoise emailed me. She had received word that there was a delom in Paro, the next valley over, about a ninety-minute drive from Thimphu. Would I be at all interested to join her for an interview? What happened next is now our shared history.

Our mutual interest in shining a spotlight on these remarkable women led us to more interviews with more women shamanic practitioners, broadening our scope to explore the larger world of divine messengers active in Bhutan today. Our goal of writing a book that we envisioned would be about the vanishing deloms soon had to be reassessed after we discovered, in fact, that deloms were proliferating though transforming in their roles and changing in their practices.

But before exploring the stories of these shifting roles, it is a good idea to take a deeper dive into the world of the deloms in Bhutan and to attempt to grasp some of the essentials of Vajrayana Buddhism relating to the deloms before introducing other types of divine messengers, to generally have some background before being introduced to the other women.

KARMA

To understand the delom's role a little better it is important to clear up the meaning of the word *karma*, perhaps one of the most persistently misused and misinterpreted terms in the modern world. In the Western way of seeing things, we live one life. In the Tibetan conception of the universe, we live multiple lives that follow each other in succession. In this view, who we are in this current life is a result of our past lives, and how we live our present life will influence our future life.

Buddhists consider the theory of karma in this way: No matter how tragic your life is, keeping in mind that this life is the retribution for your past lives, you can still find your own way; no one is impeding you, you don't have any excuses, and no one else is to blame for your actions. The way you react to the life you are handed is entirely up to you.

The bodhisattva, a buddha-to-be or a person of extraordinary compassion and spiritual achievement, is there to guide you out of your difficulties. But you are fully responsible for what you do with what is handed to you in life.

Some explain karma as being like the hand you are dealt in a game of cards. You learn how to work with the cards you're given, for yourself and for your own needs. But ultimately, whether intentionally or not, you play your hand on behalf of all sentient beings. Every one of us has karma, our own story throughout which our cards are dealt.

The consequences of our choices are nowhere more clearly delineated than in the image known as the Wheel of Life. Depicted in plain folk style paintings that speak directly to the pragmatic nature of local villagers of Bhutan, it decorates the outside of almost every Buddhist temple. Drawn for the benefit of practitioners who may not be able to read, the colorful and detailed painting is a graphic representation of what happens to people after they die. It shows how actions on earth affect the outcome of a person after death and includes depictions of the eighteen hells and people suffering in them, the punishment according to the crime.

The outer rim is divided into twelve scenes, starting with a blind person and ending with a corpse being carried. These are the interdependent causes and effects that lead to rebirth.

The outer wheel is divided into six sections, representing the six realms of existence. In the bottom right is the realm of the hungry ghosts, who can eat but never swallow, stuck in an eternal purgatory of never being fulfilled, shivering without clothes. This realm is for people who have been misers. The bottom middle section is the hell realm, where piles of people are crying out from boiling pots or are freezing in ice. To the bottom left is the realm of animals, content in their ignorance and unaware of other possibilities. Above the animals is the realm of human life—the only part of the wheel where one might find enlightenment if one actually seeks it, since this is the only place in the wheel that holds a relative balance of suffering, pleasure, and self-awareness. Moving clockwise, at the top of the Wheel of Life is the realm of gods providing the illusion of eternal happiness, but from which you can slide if you are proud or vain. Finally, there is the realm of the demigods who fight among themselves and with the gods, blinded by their own jealousy and envy. Yet in each of these realms, there is a buddha representing the possibility for beings to be saved from the cycle of rebirths and reach enlightenment.

The innermost circle of the Wheel of Life depicts the three poisons: greed, anger, and ignorance, represented respectively by a rooster, a snake, and a pig. These poisons drive our actions and reactions, with their cause and effect being karma. And it is karma that dictates through which realms we cycle. The layer of the wheel between the three poisons and the six realms is black and white. It illustrates karma very clearly to the observer: The white path leads us to escape samsara, the cycle of rebirth to achieve enlightenment. The dark path leads us back to the land of the hungry ghosts, the hell realms, or the animal realm. This is our choice based on the karma we create through our actions.

A terrifying face of a beast is above the wheel, holding it from behind and grasping it with its claws. That's the Lord of Death, whose job it is to oversee the hell realms, to determine the location for one's reincarnations, and to generally watch over the relationship between life, death, and what lies beyond for each of us. He is also the symbol of impermanence.

At the top right corner is Buddha, looking over the entirety of it all, dwelling in a state of nirvana, outside the cycle of samsara. No judgment, no wrath or pointing fingers of blame. It's all up to you.

Reading the recitations of the deloms in their biographies reveals a close connection to the *Bardo Thodrol*, known in the West as the

Tibetan Book of the Dead. In fact it's possible that this book may have served as a model for the deloms' description of the *bardo,* the place where we transit between our lives.

Bardo Thodrol, conveniently subtitled *The Treatise of the Spontaneous Liberation through Devotion of the Peaceful and Wrathful Deities,* is part of an enormous work of which Western translations offer only a small part. It is included in the collection of texts called *The Peaceful and Wrathful Deities according to Karma Lingpa* (known in Tibetan as the *Karling zhitro*), which were discovered by the religious treasure discoverer, or *terton,* Karma Lingpa sometime in the second half of the fourteenth century in southeastern Tibet. Treasure discoverers are religious people, mostly from the Nyingma sect, who, by happenstance or intent, come across treasures—texts, relics, or other things that help Buddhism in one way or another. And the *Bardo Thodrol* was found by one of these.

This collection covers the passage through the bardo, the peaceful and wrathful deities encountered by the person who is dying, and all the liturgical aspects of the mortuary rituals. In their introduction to the first English-language version of the book, Lama Kazi Samdrup and Walter Evans-Wentz explained the process of passing through the bardo and its different stages:

> From the moment of death and during three and a half days or four one believes that the "Consciousness" or the principle of consciousness of ordinary beings rests in a state of sleep or trance, without knowing that it is separated from its human body. This period of the first bardo is called the Chikhai bardo or "The Intermediate State of the Moment of Death" where first the Clear Light in its primordial purity. Then if they have perceived but are incapable of rebirth . . . he perceives this light obscured by karma which is its second aspect. When the first bardo is ended, the "Consciousness" will awaken to the understanding that he is dead and the second bardo will begin called "Chonyid bardo," or "The Intermediate

State of the Experience of Reality." This state is found in the third bardo, called Sid pai bardo or the "Intermediate State of Looking for Rebirth" which ends the moment that the principle consciousness takes rebirth in the human realm, in another realm or in a paradise. The "Consciousness" is the principle consciousness, which escapes the mortal body, transmigrates through the bardo and takes rebirth.[6]

This same term is used by the delom to describe that which travels through the world beyond. In effect, the idea of a "consciousness principle" is a Tibetan Buddhist idea that has been superimposed on pre-Buddhist Himalayan ideas of a "vital principle" or "soul," which every individual possesses.

This is heady stuff. It's complicated to think about, but the basic idea is that there is a road map that was created by Buddhists over time to direct people in their journey into the afterlife, that may or may not take a turn into the hell realm. If they have found their way into the hell realm due to misdeeds during their life, then there are doorways to get back out, and the delom hold the keys.

3

WHO ARE DELOMS?

Who are deloms? Why do they exist? What is their purpose? Do they play a role in their community, or are they simply just dear little oddities, relics of an ancient and misty past?

Deloms are unique among shamans. No other shamanic practitioners have taught Buddhist precepts in the way that deloms have. Although there is not sufficient information to trace their exact history over the past several centuries, it is possible to deduce from what's known that deloms probably arose from a confluence of beliefs from different populations. These include pre-Buddhist Tibetan beliefs. The roots of the delom can also be traced in part to both Indian and Chinese influences, though it's also likely that their origin could be found among the indigenous beliefs of Inner Asia, where shamans are known to have practiced trips to the realm of the dead. It's a tradition that stretches back hundreds of years and in Bhutan can be traced at least back to the seventeenth century.

Since deloms deal in the practice of compassion and serve people who come to them for assistance, the bodhisattva of compassion, Avalokiteshvara, is their main devotional deity and spiritual guide. A couple of rungs below Avalokiteshvara in importance are the local deities of the region, which communicate through other types of divine messengers. Ap Chundu, Ap Gem, and Jomo are the three local deities in Bhutan that speak through the shamans we interviewed, but there are hundreds of deities that are on the same level as these three.

In Bhutan deloms are only women as far as we can tell, and this could be due to several factors. Traditionally, women did not have much access to the monasteries, and even for those who did, the nunneries did not offer a high religious education. Any woman who had a leaning toward a spiritual life could only experience it on the margins. Considering the situation of the delom is a glimpse into understanding how someone who is traditionally marginalized and doesn't have institutional authority to be a teacher can nevertheless hold spiritual power in their community.

While the average person might view lamas as unreachable and too respected to be burdened with questions about mundane concerns, deloms are common village women, and it is largely thanks to their approachability that they can bring the teachings of Buddha directly to the people in a way that the monastic establishment cannot.

On the whole, deloms are not literate, although some can read prayers. Deloms are not considered to be elevated above other community members in any way nor in a position that threatens those in power. They're simply the messengers of the Lord of the Dead, after all, and so people of all stripes can consult them without subverting any power structures. They remain simple village women as they provide their crucial service of linking people with firsthand knowledge of the remarkable hell realms, in the process cementing the practice of Buddhism ever more firmly in their community.

The folk character of deloms, and a certain wariness from the monastic establishment, plus the fact that deloms don't wear any obvious religious robes, give clues to their existence on the fringes of Buddhist culture. Some believe that the tradition of the delom is pre-Buddhist and that they transformed into their current form with the arrival of Buddhism, but this gets into murky waters; although knowledge on pre-Buddhist beliefs has progressed in the last fifty years, the information about them is still sparse and subject to different theories.

All that can be said for certain is that an assimilation and integration of these beliefs and practices into Buddhism took place. But there is so far no known proof that deloms existed as part of pre-Buddhist practices. However, the term *delom* does not have an equivalent in Sanskrit or in Chinese, and it does not have any particular Buddhist connotations either. So perhaps this indicates that it arose from the indigenous Tibetan culture.

What we do know is this: The process that enabled deloms to merge into Buddhist societies without conserving the memory of their origins is not unique in Tibetan culture, where many pre-Buddhist beliefs and practices, sometimes called shamanic, have survived by being assimilated into Buddhism. When it arrived in Tibet in the seventh century, Buddhism encountered a set of indigenous beliefs whose principal foundations were in total disagreement with its own, such as worshipping deities living in nature who had to be placated and who gave power and strength to humans, who performed animal sacrifices and had no concept of karma or reincarnation. Instead of having a "consciousness principle" that migrates when one dies in Buddhism, pre-Buddhist beliefs often had simply a "vital principle" that dies with the body. The subsequent centuries witnessed a struggle between the adherents of these indigenous beliefs and the Buddhist missionaries throughout the Himalayas, who eventually transformed and incorporated certain elements of these indigenous beliefs into local Buddhist belief and practices.

Pre-Buddhist beliefs were absorbed into Buddhism and the ancient religion was no longer mentioned. As Anne Marie Blondeau points out, "When in the end Buddhism triumphed definitively, it removed from the memories of the Tibetans any memory of a religion that it held in check."[7]

Traveling to the land of the dead was already a familiar idea to Buddhists: prestigious figures such as Avalokiteshvara and Maudgalyana, a disciple of Buddha, had descended into the hell realms; in China, stories were recorded of ordinary people who went to the hell realms by mistake and returned to the world. Regardless of the delom's origins, Buddhism recast the idea into its own way of explaining things. And while shamanic traces remain in deloms, the Buddhist assimilation is complete. The biographies of deloms, which start to appear from the twelfth century in Tibet, were propagating Buddhist teachings but did not mention that deloms could make multiple journeys to the netherworld. They were more closely modeled after the great Buddhist saints. They showed how reality could be manipulated in order to propagate a Buddhist view and how lived reality continued to be bent to support a cause.

Today, the deloms are accepted on some level by members of the Buddhist clergy, but it is probably due to the religious ambiguity of deloms that the monastic establishment has often been inconsistent about accepting them. Nevertheless, deloms have persisted without disappearing over the centuries; they are witnesses to a largely lost worldview and disseminators—among others—of the Buddhist ideology that overtook the Himalayan world.

THE CONNECTING LINK

To understand the role of the deloms, it's best to start back at the traditional Buddhist monastery. In Bhutan the Buddhist monastic body is largely male and sequestered, inhabited by men who have left behind the rest of the world to take up the study of the Buddha's teachings. They shave their heads and give up their regular clothes for the maroon robes of devout monkhood. From a young age, they learn to read and write in Classical Tibetan; they study, recite mantras, and perform rituals on behalf of all sentient beings. It is the life of a cloister, withdrawn from regular daily activities in order to work toward enlightenment. However, some of them eventually quit the monastery, deciding instead to return to the life of a layman.

Between the monastery and the community there are the *gomchens*, lay practitioners who help interpret the texts and aid regular laypeople along a devout path. They set community standards of decency and moral behavior, in addition to performing rituals for individuals and generally supporting the work of the monks.

Deloms as people are not separate from the daily life of the common people: they are themselves common women, part of their communities, who are easily sought out and approached. The thread that bound together the monastery, the gomchens, and the delom was a form of writing that emerged as something completely separate from anything at all like a religious text. It was a kind of writing that had never been seen before. These were the delom biographies.

4

DELOM BIOGRAPHIES

Delom "biographies" tell the story of the story of the life of one who has traveled to the netherworld. But actually, the word *biography* is a misnomer. Many, or maybe all, of these were written by monks for the sole purpose of recounting the lives of these women in relationship to Buddhist teachings, with little or no discussion of the delom's worldly life.

There have been numerous delom biographies written over time, and every delom biography is remarkably similar to the others, so similar, in fact, that one might assume that is the intent. That is to say, if a delom has the exact otherworldly experience of other deloms, and is able to recount it in exactly the same way, that essentially shores up the veracity of their experience. But beyond the simple existence of these biographies there are several clues within them that clearly indicate the deloms did in fact really exist in the past. Although they don't get into any great details, delom biographies do usually give information about their birthplace, their parents' names, and their social background, but, very often, they omit the year of their birth or the year of their delom experience. Generally speaking, the biographies really get going the moment the delom leaves her body to travel the hell realms, and they dive deepest into the detailed experiences and encounters that she has.

Deloms also appear in Himalayan historical literature, and these few literary references provide valuable historical clues. Combined with the information from the biographies, it is possible to both confirm that deloms were indeed historical persons and to attempt to date both the first occurrence of the phenomenon and the earliest appearance of delom biographies.

With the exception of the biography of Nangsa Obum in the twelfth century, the delom literary genre really appears to blossom in the sixteenth century. From the biographies, it is known that deloms were predominantly from the Nyingma and Kagyu schools of Buddhism. This is not a great surprise since these two schools give a good deal of importance to mysticism and allow some latitude in practice. Between the twelfth and fifteenth centuries, these two schools of Buddhism nurtured intellectual and religious movements that supported the formation of the delom literary genre.

One of the dominant aspects of the delom stories is the place given to the worship of Avalokiteshvara (Chenrezig in Tibetan), the bodhisattva who saves beings, the embodiment of compassion. The deloms see themselves as his incarnations, and OM MANI PADME HUM (HRIH)—a mantra of six or seven syllables—punctuates the narratives throughout. This mantra of Avalokiteshvara is said to have the power to save one from the hell realms.

Just to clarify, we have been speaking here about historical deloms—women (and very rarely also men), who lived in the Tibetan cultural world centuries ago. But deloms still exist in Bhutan. We have met them and interviewed them. Although the delom practice is currently changing and expanding into different roles, it very much still exists.

Many of the women you are going to meet in this book may or may not qualify as deloms in the historical sense of the term. This book is in part about our discovery of the evolution of the modern delom. And while deloms are found all throughout the Himalayan region, this book concentrates strictly on deloms and delom practice in Bhutan.

THE TRADITION OF DELOM BIOGRAPHIES

As I mentioned, we assume that the historical biographies of Himalayan deloms were written by monks, who were the only people educated enough to undertake such a task. Monks also understood the value of the deloms' teachings in reinforcing Buddhism, and by writing these official biographies they strengthened the delom's position in Buddhist society. Or, it's always possible that deloms themselves retold their experiences to a literate person, a scribe, who then put them into the form of a story. Either way, it's likely that a biography was written just after the death of the delom when her memory was still very much alive and her story well-known among the local people. In fact, some delom biographies are written as a part of a longer, more general biography of a religious person's life, and only through reading the longer biography do you find out that the person had a delom experience.

Altogether, we aren't sure how many individual biographies there are. Some biographies have several versions, and almost certainly not all have survived until today. Not counting the multiple versions of one delom's biography, there are a total of at least fifteen that we know about from Tibet, Bhutan, and Nepal.

There are likely more.

The delom biographies are like the histories of saints: they are archives of a religious experience that a woman has had. Interestingly, while the Buddhist leadership considers the delom biographies to be authoritative regarding the information they contain, they would not necessarily consider the same information told by a living delom to be authoritative. Perhaps this is a reflection of a common human phenomenon: religious authorities often don't recognize saints or other people with mystical experiences as having genuine experiences while they are still alive, and only occasionally recognize their authenticity after death. If that's the case, the lack of recognition might not be because they're women but could be simply because their experiences are considered unorthodox.

Since the bulk of a delom biography is devoted to what the delom did and saw while she was in the hells, and her main Buddhist message to the living to live an ethical and spiritual life, we learn little to nothing about the actual life of the deloms themselves from these texts. We can only piece together that information based on other historical sources. It's as if their lives were completely static in the stories. There's also never a description of how they die—they simply cover themselves and they go. The "how" remains shrouded in mystery.

Because the biographies convey their journey to the hell realms as a onetime thing, it could be interpreted as an extensive and very detailed dream rather than a shamanic experience. Seen in that light, the delom biographies just become fantastic, again, like Christian saints who go into a rapture and see the body of Christ or have transformative experiences—ones that could easily be reinterpreted as dreams or some other kind of hallucination.

I think about what life must have been like four centuries ago for these very extraordinary women who lived in the quiet forests and on the small farms along the rivers that wind through the high mountains of Bhutan. The delom Sangay Choezom was one of those women, and it was her biography that Françoise translated and that we have included in the third part of this book. I ponder all the details of her life that have been so carefully omitted from that text, and build an image from a mess of clues. We know what her home valley is like now, and we have historical knowledge of what life was like at that time. There are many strands of life in rural Bhutan that have continued unbroken from that time into present day. Weaving together what Françoise has described to me, and from the other clues I've assembled, I can begin to imagine who this woman was and how she lived.

THE DELOM SANGAY CHOEZOM

Sangay Choezom was an ordinary rural woman. Short and stout, her body would have been strong from the daily hard work of managing a farm, her powerful legs accustomed to climbing the steep foothills of the Himalayas that surrounded her family's home. Her straight black hair would be cut short, fringing her face, and she would wear a full kira—a length of woven cloth intricately folded into a full length dress and pinned at the shoulders with elaborate silver pins—over which she would have worn a *toego*—a waist-length jacket. This is the traditional dress for Bhutanese women that has remained almost entirely unchanged over the past several centuries.

Sangay shared her home with her siblings, parents, and grand-parents in eastern Bhutan, near Trashigang, sometime in the late seventeenth or early eighteenth century. Like the other houses on the field, her family's house was made of wood and bamboo and stood on stilts with a bamboo floor. As was true for everyone in her region, her family were farmers. They grew almost all the food they needed and traded for the rest. The fields would have been planted with millet and radishes, and chickens would have been kept for eggs. Although they would have raised cattle, ox, and pigs, they didn't eat much meat. In the lean season, her father was a cattle trader, who might have walked as far as Tibet or India to find markets.

Nestled deep in a valley at an elevation of about 1,200 meters, Sangay Choezom's family home was likely one of several houses scattered across a large field. Surrounded by the lowland subtropical forest that is typical of southeastern Bhutan, the borders of the field would have been encroached upon by the lowland bamboo and lemongrass that grows at this altitude replacing the pines and other evergreens of the higher mountains. Monkeys, tigers, boars, and deer would have roamed these woods outside their little valley and been chased away from the cattle and crops by diligent farmers. At that time, Trashigang would have been accessible by a trail to what is now India and at that time was the kingdom of Assam. If Sangay walked through the jungle for a week she would have arrived in that neighboring kingdom. Her family was likely religious. There would have been a small altar in the corner of the main room of their home.

Religious education for Sangay Choezom's family would have come from the gomchens, or Buddhist lay practitioners. These were village men who studied religious texts and rituals with a master and were exempted from farmwork during their studies. Some of the gomchens were easy to spot because they did not cut their hair for the entire duration of their studies, and under their long, flowing black hair, white woven garments embellished with scarlet woven bands. The others just wore a longer *gho*, the traditional men's garment in Bhutan, which looks a bit like a Japanese kimono, sewn of red cloth and worn with a maroon scarf.

The gomchens served as interpreters of Buddhist teachings for the farmers of the area, and they led rituals in the community. They were a necessary link between the monastic body of Buddhism and the people, because the monastery was difficult to access for a normal layperson. Drametse, a Nyingma monastery, would have been the closest monastery to Sangay Choezom's home, and it might have taken one day or even two to walk there. There is a chance that Sangay Choezom actually went to Drametse at some point.

So in her surroundings there were both monks in the monastery as well as gomchens living among the people in the villages. Of greater significance than the geographical distance was the distance between the body of monks who were able to read and recite in Classical Tibetan and the largely illiterate population outside the monastery.

Sangay Choezom seems to have been an average Bhutanese woman of her time, but in fact she lived a far from average life. Her daily life was very likely to have been inconveniently interrupted by serious illness, fainting spells, and trances, typical to deloms, culminating eventually in a prolonged "death" during which she apparently left her body. Her family had already received warnings about this possibility, so her body was kept warm in preparation for her eventual return.

And return she did. After Sangay Choezom came back to her body and awoke among her family, she recounted to them what had happened. She had made a trip to the hell realms, she explained, where she was met by the Lord of the Dead himself, known to the Bhutanese as Shinje Chogyel or Yama Dharmaraja. He explained to her how the hells worked and what the living could do to alleviate the suffering of those trapped there, as well as how to avoid being trapped there altogether. Shinje Chogyel also pointed out to her the relatives of her neighbors and friends so that she could bring back messages to their families in the land of the living, letting them know how to help their suffering—put up one hundred prayer flags, for example, or complete one hundred thousand prostrations. She witnessed the suffering that awaited people who committed particular sins, such as excessively eating meat or torturing animals. These were very practical lessons in what would occur if such actions continued unabated.

When this happened—when Sangay Choezom left her body, visited the hell realms, was guided through them by the Lord of the Dead, and returned to the living—this was the moment of time that transformed her from being an average farm woman to becoming a delom.

PART TWO

INHABITING A HUMAN BODY: MODERN DIVINE MESSENGERS IN BHUTAN

5

NAMING NAMES

When Françoise and I embarked on our interviews, we hoped to find maybe one more delom to talk to. We started to ask around: who knew if there were any deloms in western Bhutan? People would answer they knew about a *rizam*, or they had heard about a *nyenjum*. Some had heard there was one woman who was even a *khandrom*.

We were confused, but we thought maybe the people talking to us were confused by what we were asking. We thought that perhaps what we knew as delom were now being called by a whole host of other names. We set out to interview as many women as we could in the short time we had available, assuming it would be a few days of interviews at best. With the time it takes to travel the winding mountain roads that are the signature of Bhutan, we ended up on a journey of two weeks' duration that would in the end take us throughout western Bhutan, and which would show us that we had barely scratched the surface.

What we learned is that the women we thought of as deloms in the traditional sense are indeed sparse, but other similar types of female shamans are proliferating. Was there a relationship between the other practitioners and the women we, as outsiders, called deloms? We asked each of the shamans we met to help us to define their designation through explaining their work and their roles in the community. Were there lots of different kinds of unrelated shamanic practices going on, or were they all somehow different forms of the core practice of the deloms?

As we inquired, we gathered all these definitions together. The story told here is what we learned: what these women told us about who they are, what they do in relation to each other, and what they do in relation to the deities. In truth, the lines that defined the semantic boundaries between each of them were never very clear. In fact, the roles, work, and social status of these women are fluid and almost always overlapping. What we probably naively thought of as definitions over time turned into general guidelines. The delom has transformed into rizam, rizam into khandrom, and separate but related is nyenjom. In the end we decided to call them by the terms they were using themselves and to tell their stories as they were told to us.

Reincarnating Rizams

While traveling in western Bhutan we didn't hear about too many "deloms," but we often heard about "rizams," a term defined as "a lady of good extraction." In reality, the rizams we met were much more than ladies of good extraction. Because of their unusual duties, rizams were distinguished from other villagers, even though they were still outranked by monks as well as by the village leaders. As it turns out, "rizam" always implies a religious practitioner, and it seems to be a purely Bhutanese term not often used in Tibet. In Sangay Choezom's biography Avalokiteshvara addresses her in Tibetan as a "woman of good extraction."

From the interviews we made there emerged an extraordinary difference between a rizam and the delom. A rizam is essentially a delom once removed: a reincarnated delom. In Vajrayana Buddhism, someone who attains enlightenment during their lifetime does not need to return to the cycle of death and rebirth of samsara when they die. Yet there are some who choose to do so in order to benefit beings and are given the special title of "rinpoche" or "tulku," and they are mostly men. It turned out that the rizams of western Bhutan are quite the same. They are reincarnations of previous deloms. As a reincarnation, a rizam is a reflection of her original delom. She hasn't traveled to the hells herself. Instead, she inherits the knowledge of that journey through the hell realms from the original delom, her previous incarnation. In other words, the delom did the work of dying and traveling to the hell realms, and now the rizam receives the teachings from that experience without having to make that trip herself.

One of the ways that a reincarnated lama, called a tulku or rinpoche, is identified is by exhibiting the same actions, reciting the same prayers, and recognizing the religious belongings of the previous incarnation. As part of the identification, the child lama has to recognize the objects of the previous lama or to recite prayers that they wouldn't necessarily know, except for the fact that they are an incarnation of that previous lama. Senior lamas are trained to recognize these clues to identify incarnations. This is the same system that is used to identify a future Dalai Lama.

The situation is similar for a rizam. She might have a vision of something that belonged to the previous delom or maybe have a vision about previous delom's village even if she's never been there. But there is no authoritative system for recognizing rizams as reincarnations of deloms. Senior lamas might be experts in identifying tulkus or rinpoches, but they know nothing about previous deloms of whom a rizam might be a reincarnation. A rizam is like a mirror of the Buddhist reincarnated lamas, but in a completely different realm—a place where the monastic establishment does not have any foothold. Instead, when asked, they might say the deity or previous incarnation will reveal itself over time. In other words, there is no standardized way that the monastic establishment can recognize a rizam. Regular social norms cannot operate in her world. No religious authority tells a rizam that she is the reincarnation of a particular delom of the past. They realize themselves that they are the reincarnation.

Interestingly, all three rizams we met in western Bhutan were incarnations of a single delom: Namgay Choezom, who has no known written biography, at least that we know about. Namgay Choezom traveled to the hells, and now the modern-day rizams, who are spared that journey, are able to gain knowledge of the hells from her experience as recalled through them. Because of their previous delom incarnation, rizams remember the hells. They also perform different divinations in order to help people solve problems in their regular daily lives. Divinations are a kind of deeper look into a situation, or into the future, using different tools for reading the answer. Sometimes rice is thrown in the air, and the pattern it makes is then read. Sometimes dice are thrown, and the numbers tell their own story.

The rizam we met in Punakha gave us this definition: "*Rizam* is derived from *rig zang*, which means a person of high-class or an emanation of a delom of high-class." *Rizam* means "one of high birth," she said. Early on, she recalled, she had been called a nyenjom, who are able to become possessed by local deities. When rizams first appeared in Bhutan, she explained, the deities of the nyenjoms could not possess the rizams and were unable to speak through the rizam at all. In this way, Namgay Choezom subdued and converted five of the pawos, male mediums, and nyenjoms, female mediums. Once she converted them, this elevated their status, and these nyenjoms and pawos were then called rizams, after her title.

It is said that when this rizam went to subdue these mediums, they feared her, became numb, and could not even talk. Some were subdued just by her presence. She explained to us that it was during one of her teachings that she instructed people to call her "rizam" rather than "nyenjom," when she realized that she was an incarnation of the delom Namgay Choezom.

The rizams' role serves the dual purpose of giving the world outside the monastery religious teachings and continuing to provide modern Bhutanese with access to spiritual guidance in a way that's easily understood. Although rizams are a whole different class of reincarnates that exist entirely outside the monastery, there's the exceptional case of Ani Rizam from Paro, who leads a religious life, hence her title "Ani," which means nun. Her son is a tulku and the leader of the monastery where she lives. She told us that the title "Rizam" was given to Namgay Choezom, a delom who lived a long time ago, so the villagers began to call Namgay Choezom's incarnations "rizam" and do so until today. Thus, according to Ani Rizam, it was Namgay Choezom herself who introduced the term rizam in Bhutan.

Ani Rizam also told us that it's acceptable to call a rizam a "khandrom" by virtue of the fact that she is the emanation of a previous khandrom. When a delom becomes enlightened she becomes a khandrom, so the rizams who are incarnations of Namgay Choezom could also be called "khandrom"—a very exalted term. Nevertheless, these women generally call themselves "rizam" because they consider themselves foremost to be an incarnation of a previous delom. But there are always exceptions to every rule, and we found one exception in a self-proclaimed khandrom.

SKY-GOERS

Khandrom, or *khandroma* in Tibetan, is the translation of the Sanskrit *dakini*, "a sky-goer," and refers to a female deity important in the Vajrayana. Interestingly, over time the definition of khandrom has expanded to mean one who is born to help sentient beings and has attained some form of enlightenment. It is often used to refer to the female consorts of male lamas. In the eighth century, Khandrom Yeshe Tsogyal and Khandrom Mandarava were the consorts of Padmasambhava, the bringer of Buddhism to Bhutan. Khandrom Sonam Peldon was the consort of the saint Phajo Drugom Zhigpo in the thirteenth century. It is believed that all of them—both saints and their consorts—were consciously born to help sentient beings. Even if they appear in human form, they are not earthly beings.

Generally, it is an honorific term given to women. The wife of a high lama or *thogden* (yogi), for example, is referred to as that lama's khandrom; her authority seems to be derived partly through her association with her partner, but she is also an elevated partner in her own right whose realization is usually recognized by her partner. Both lamas and yogis are religious figures who can marry if they have not taken a vow of celibacy, and in Vajrayana Buddhism a female consort is essential to progress on the path of enlightenment. A khandrom is considered to be a spiritually advanced female practitioner capable of assisting her partner in his meditation. She has nothing to do with worldly deities, and her special power is her Buddhist enlightened nature. However, in Bhutan, by extension and out of respect, people address most women of a certain religious status as khandrom.

Mediums of the Local Deities

Rizams, and by extension those rizams who are also called khandrom, are in almost all ways quite different from the nyenjoms. The nyenjoms are the local mediums in western Bhutan and are connected with the mundane deities of the locality and their particular area. Although the strict meaning of the word *nyenjom* is *yogini*, it is not an elevated term, and in Bhutan, it refers to women who worship, pacify, and perform rituals for the local deities. Nyenjoms are known for being able to heal people who are possessed by unenlightened deities. Nyenjoms themselves are also possessed by such deities, which gives the deities the power to speak through the nyenjom.

Nyenjom is a term used exclusively in western Bhutan and Sikkim. In other regions of Bhutan the equivalent term is *pamo*, which is also used in Arunachal Pradesh in India and parts of Tibet. In western Bhutan, male mediums are less common than female mediums and are called pawos as they are in the rest of Bhutan.

Nyenjoms perform rituals to placate the local deities and make sure that they don't do any harm in their communities. The specific rituals of the nyenjom are not considered Buddhist—in Bhutan they are associated with Bon beliefs, although the nyenjoms consider themselves to be Buddhist.

Nyenjoms are very much associated with the rituals and practices of the local deities who take possession of their bodies. These local deities are pre-Buddhist spirits who have been subdued by a Buddhist saint and have pledged to protect Buddhism. These deities are placed on the lowest rung of the pantheon ladder of Bhutanese deities. Because they are the protector of a region of land, they live in the mountains, which allows them to protect the people in a community. And because they have been transformed into protectors of Buddhism by a saint, it is acceptable to worship them and make offerings on certain days.

These are just the barest sketches of the types of female shamans we present here and whose roles and lives overlap and intermingle.

6

THE SKY-GOER OF PARO

As Françoise wheeled our Toyota Land Cruiser along the winding highway from Thimphu to Paro, she told me that the woman we were about to meet seemed to be an unusual delom. She was puzzled. She had heard that this delom was also called "khandrom."

As we drove to her house, we pondered this a little more. Was "khandrom" actually bestowed upon her by someone or had she decided on it herself?

It was a cloudy April afternoon in 2011 when Françoise and I made our way to a traditional farmhouse standing in the middle of the paddy fields of the Paro valley. Françoise parked the car on the side of the dirt road in front of the house, and we walked along a path between two newly planted rice paddies full of green shoots in even rows up to the wooden steps of the house.

While on the road we had bought some offerings of juice and different sweet snacks, and we now carried these along with the customary monetary offering. A young man sat silently examining us from the wooden porch at the top of the steps. We stopped at the bottom of the steps, and Françoise asked him if this was the home of the delom. "Indeed, it is," he replied, and after considering us for a few more seconds, he went inside to search for her. A few minutes later we were led into the main room of the house. The broad planks of the wooden floors were smoothed from years of use. The plastered walls were painted a pale yellow. We were invited to sit on some wool cushions on the floor, next to what looked like a tall wooden chair, a raised platform similar to a monk's seat at a temple. The delom entered and took her seat on the chair. Françoise spoke to her in Dzongkha, her native tongue, telling her that we heard she was a khandrom.

She told us that in fact she was the only khandrom in Bhutan, as she was the only one to be recognized by the Je Khenpo, who is the head of the Drukpa lineage, and so the main religious authority in Bhutan. She further explained that there are many fake khandroms and that generally people don't understand the difference.

While lamas teach through books and through other spiritual techniques, she explained, a khandrom's teaching is through the mind. She said that a khandrom can also make predictions, which she does by simply looking at someone's face. Through a person's face she sees their mind, and by looking at their mind she can tell what she needs to tell them. That is the capacity of the khandrom, she concluded, a skill that, apparently, she alone had.

She told us that, in times past, there was a belief that a khandrom who had a husband and a child wasn't a real khandrom. But, she pointed out, Phajo Drugom Zhigpo, the Tibetan Buddhist master who first introduced the Drukpa Kagyu sect to Bhutan in the thirteenth century, and his consort, Sonam Peldren, had seven sons. Sonam Peldren was a khandrom, she continued, and so she is a clear example that one can have children and be a khandrom.

The delom was in her late thirties. She told us she was born in the year of the Dragon, so maybe 1976. For some reason I had imagined that she was going to be much older than that. She asked us why we were visiting her, and Françoise asked her to tell us the story of her life.

She recalled that her father came from a good religious family here in Paro and that he was from a Drukpa lineage. Her mother was also from a good family, but her parents had died when she was thirteen. Around the age of eleven she started to become sick. Her parents didn't understand what was wrong with her. All she wanted to do was practice religion. At fourteen, after the death of her parents, she got married, and by the age of eighteen she had two children. Back then she didn't particularly like married life, and she didn't particularly like raising children. Nowadays, she said, her former husband looks after the children. She didn't really even want to talk about them. Finally, she left her family to undertake a long period of meditation, and when she finished her meditation, she received a prophecy to remarry. So now she has another child from her second husband.

She told us that all of these things happened—the marriage, the children, the remarriage—because of her past lives. In her previous life she was a delom in Wangdue Phodrang in the Shar district of western Bhutan, she explains.

When she was twenty-four years old, she died for a week. While she was dead, she was unconscious but she could see that everybody around her was crying. She left her body and went to the hells and there she met her *yidam*, or tutelary deity, Vajrayogini, a khandrom of the highest level. Vajrayogini showed her the hells. She did not realize she was dead until she saw that she had no shadow, she told us. She saw the eighteen hells and was very scared.

Then, she told us, she arrived at a plain that she described as being "as flat as the airport." There she saw Shinje Chogyel, the Lord of Death, who explained everything to her and told her to go back to earth to propagate what she had seen. The black demon who takes count of the bad deeds was also down in the hells. He really frightened her, she said.

Suddenly a wind and fog kicked up, and she came back to earth where everybody started calling her "khandrom." But, she told us, there were obstacles. After she had returned to her body, she went to see the young Gyalsey Tulku, a very high Drukpa reincarnate lama who resided in the Tango monastery, which is in the forest in the Thimphu valley. He understood her, she said, because he himself had been a sickly child, but he was still too young to be able to give her advice about what had happened to her. She went to see the Je Khenpo, the head abbot of Bhutan, who told her that she was a khandrom and should practice religion. He advised her to go and meet with the Dorje Lopen, the religious master of the monastic body and just below the Je Khenpo in rank, and he gave her religious instructions. The Je Khenpo then named her Khandrom

Yeshe Drolma, which means the Tara, the female Buddha and goddess of compassion.

After that, she was no longer sick. She understood that she had to stay away from pollution and remain in a clean environment, so now she hardly goes to other people's houses. People are disturbing the deities, she said, by polluting their bodies. She follows a strict diet: no garlic, no onion, no pork, no fish, no eggs, and only a little bit of dry beef. She decided to build her own house partly to be able to stay pure. She told us that she never attends events where large crowds gather. The Paro Tsechu is the main religious festival of her area, attended by hundreds of people over the course of several days. The main event is the unfurling of a massive sacred scroll painted with an image of Guru Rinpoche. Pilgrims come from across Bhutan just to be in the presence of the scroll when it is at last revealed. Over the course of the several days, sacred dances are performed by the monks who inhabit the monastery at Paro. Outside the fortress gates of the monastery, it feels like a country fair: families meet up with each other, spending the days and nights camping out together, and all kinds of socializing ensues. The Khandrom told us that to avoid impurities she now watches the Paro Tsechu on TV.

Despite her now isolated life, she is able to advise people, especially women, she says, since she has gone through the whole cycle of life and can understand the problems of other women. Her main advice to those who seek her out is to keep good hygiene and to keep everything clean. She tells us that she has completely embraced the Buddhist way, but on the fifteenth day of every month, a special day in the Buddhist calendar, she does not feel well.

She has never returned to the hells since her first visit there.

We made our way out the door where the young man was once again sitting and another young woman was was waiting there, ready to see the Khandrom.

7

THE LOCAL DEITIES' SPOKESPERSON

In April 2018 I returned to Bhutan to spend two weeks with Françoise, immersed in the world of the divine messengers. She had heard that new deloms were being identified in parts of western Bhutan, and we wanted to meet them. We also hoped to once again interview the delom in Paro, whom we had met and interviewed together years before. It had been five years since I was last in Bhutan, so for me it was also a chance to once again see and feel the place I was writing about.

Once the word got out that we were eager to find more deloms, it seemed like there was a delom, or mediums, around every bend in the road. People from all walks of life lit up in their conversations with us about the delom, nyenjom, or rizam. Their family consulted a nyenjom every year, they told us, or there was a certain rizam they would go to for advice regularly. The terms all seemed to be almost interchangeable.

The stories we heard about these women made us wonder if they fit into our understanding of deloms, if they were performing the same task that we understood deloms to perform traditionally— advising people about the fates of dead family members in negotiating the hell realms—or if they were playing some entirely other roles. It felt like so many possibilities were opening up.

Having arrived in Bhutan on a tourist visa, I was assigned a guide, whose job it was to show me the sights of the beautiful kingdom of Bhutan. The day after I arrived, still jet-lagged, Françoise and I walked down Norzin Lam, the main street in Thimphu, to the tour agency office. It was morning commute time, so the sidewalks were full of clusters of young women in perfectly pressed kira heading for their office jobs and young men in traditional gho, knee socks, and dress shoes also on their way along the road to work. The street was crammed with cars, deftly directed by a single traffic cop. When we arrived at the tour agency office, I was introduced to my guide, Chencho Dorji.

In his mid-twenties, tall and slight, Chencho was kind and eager. He told me that he was from a farming family in the Paro valley. The lucky thing about the life of a guide, he said, is that the slow season for tourism coincides with the rice harvest, so when he had time off from his work with tourists, he would head home to the farm to help with the harvest. I gave him a straightforward explanation of what I wanted to do, and Chencho jumped on board with the plan, quickly evolving from the role of tour guide into a partner and strategist in our work. In fact, he told me, even his aunt was a nyenjom. He had heard about a nyenjom who lived out in Haa valley, he said. He would make a couple of calls to find out if we could visit her. So, a few days after I arrived, Chencho, the driver, and I made our way to Haa to spend the night at a farmhouse and search out the nyenjom.

It was a beautiful drive to Haa, full of cool spring air, blossoming apple trees, new shoots in the rice and barley fields, and deep pine forests all around. Haa valley is so steep that there's not a lot of agriculture other than subsistence farming, which is done on any slope that's flat enough for an ox to pull a plow on, terraced into submission into the hillside and cut off on the edges by pine forest.

Our van followed the road through the valley as it narrowed and became a dirt track, finally pulling up to a little farmhouse set off by itself on a hill surrounded by barley fields. As we climbed out of the van we were greeted with warm smiles by Pema Dema, her husband, and Pema's twenty-something-year-old daughter. As soon as we had shed our bags in our respective rooms and returned to the kitchen, we were presented with a magnificent pile of deep-fried buckwheat *hoentey*, a specialty of Haa that are like the Himalayan dumplings called *momo*s, filled with pork and dried turnip leaves. I thoroughly and gratefully devoured mine, feeling quite proud that I had completely cleaned my plate. Every other momo I've consumed since is now measured against these hoenteys, and none have yet to compare. But the hoenteys were closely followed by a huge mound of red rice, dried pork cooked with turnips, green beans cooked with fresh cheese, chicken mixed with spices and chili, and of course endless rounds of milk tea. I didn't really stand a chance.

I tried to make up for my disappointing performance at dinner in the morning by eating my whole bowl of rice and a boiled egg and more dried pork with turnip and plenty of chili, this time mixed with fresh cheese. I thought I had done really well, actually eating my whole bowl of food, but my hostess was visibly disappointed in my eating abilities. Her low opinion changed instantly when Chencho told her that I was interested in meeting a nyenjom. She was clearly thrilled. After she and Chencho had a long conversation in Dzongkha, we all piled into the van and drove to the other side of the valley to introduce me to her nyenjom.

Hours earlier, just after dawn, I had watched as the neighbors across the road from the farmhouse began working on adding windows and a new wooden frame to a house under construction. The swirling smoke of burning juniper rose from the ceremony being performed in the midst of the construction site, consecrating this new layer of the building in progress.

The houses in Haa took a beating during the earthquake of 2011, and so there's quite a lot of new construction still going on, still building in the old rammed earth style, which costs almost no money but instead requires generations of expertise. It takes no money, that is, if you are willing to work with neighbors to dig up the mud yourself and refine it to make it smooth enough to turn into solid bricks. You then chop down the trees that you need to bring to the little sawmill to make flat, straight, solid boards that are laid between the layers of mud, strengthening the fabrication so you can continue to add more mud walls without the weight of it collapsing down on itself. And with the layer of wood you can add window frames that are produced by a master carpenter, who doubles as the architect, out of your milled wood, which are fixed down into the mud walls, traditionally without a single nail required.

That morning we made the long, slow drive back across the valley, heading out the track the way we had come in. With the steep valley wall rising on our left as we made our slow way along, the right side opened up to the fields and an occasional farmhouse. Finally, we stopped on a hillside where an innocuous little farmhouse stood directly below the road.

Tsering Pelden was old, and her bare feet were twisted from the leprosy that affected her in her childhood. Yet she got around just fine, especially considering that the path to her house consisted of a series of stone steps hand carved into a steep rock face, a wooden ladder attached to the bottom of the stone steps, the top of the ladder secured to a wooden landing, followed by a second flight of steps, wooden ones this time, that delivered you to the first level of her house.

Among the mayhem of several small children, dogs, and a beautiful little gray cat sleeping through it all, she led us into the front room of her house and proceeded to give me the details on the local deities of her particular village, including the story of a magical carpenter who had built all the houses in the village and who was an emanation of Padmasambhava. It turns out that this magical carpenter, Tulku Zowa Baley, is a famous mythical figure in Bhutan credited with the construction of many buildings.

I asked her for an explanation of what a nyenjom is, and she replied by telling the origin story of the nyenjom as she knew it. The gods sent a bird to the world, and the bird turned into a nyenjom. The nyenjom came here into the world to alleviate all suffering and to help all sentient beings, she told us. Here in Haa, she explained, all problems are due to the anger of the local protective deity that arises when the humans do not make offerings and worship him properly every year.

Tsering Pelden told me how she first discovered that she was a nyenjom after suffering years of ill health and what she called madness, which, she conceded, she should have realized much sooner since both illness and madness are obvious indications of supernatural ability.

Although her name is Tsering Pelden, her nickname is Jakam, which means "white bird." Apparently when she was a little girl she didn't speak very well. When she was eight years old, she said she thought a white bird was her mother, so people started calling her Jakam. And when people started to call her Jakam, she finally started to talk.

A few years later, when she was twelve, she was down at the river washing clothes when a crown, the specific headdress that nyenjoms wear, floated down the river toward her. She threw it to the other side, she said, but it floated back to her again, so this time she took it and kept it, but she didn't think much about it. She was still twelve when she had some kind of skin disease, and within a short time her father and mother died. She was very poor and had no one to help her.

Years went by in sickness and madness for Jakam. When she turned twenty-five, she was married but she remained sick, and at that point she assumed that the disease was caused by the water spirits, called *lu* in Dzongkha. In fact, this was a sign that she was destined to be a nyenjom, but she still didn't know that. Around the same time, she suddenly lashed out violently, hitting her husband. She left her home and took off roaming through the valley until finally she lost consciousness. When she regained consciousness, she met a Hindu astrologer who used to come to Bhutan in winter to give predictions. He told her that she was some kind of medium, but Jakam didn't understand Hindi well and therefore didn't really comprehend what the astrologer was telling her, and so she was back to square one.

Until the age of thirty-eight, Jakam had recurring bouts of madness, and strange events continued to happen. Eventually someone advised her to visit a delom, which she did. The delom proceeded to recount to Jakam her entire life story. It was in this meeting with the delom that Jakam finally realized that she was a nyenjom.

The delom told her to make offerings to the five dakinis who are in the area. After she started to make these offerings, sure enough, her suffering proceeded to diminish and people began to seek her assistance as a nyenjom.

She is used to her suffering now, she says, since as a nyenjom she has to suffer in the same way as her deity has suffered. She will remain a nyenjom until she passes away, she proclaimed. When that time comes, the next nyenjom of the region won't necessarily be her daughter. It doesn't necessarily proceed through the family.

One of her tutelary deities, whom she calls by the honorific and very Buddhist term khandrom, is in fact a local deity called Ache Gyem to whom the people of the Haa district make offerings. This is how the nyenjom recounted the story of Ache Gyem to me. There are several local deities in Haa region. Ap Chundu is the foremost local deity of Bhutan and also the main protective deity of Haa. Ap Joyak is not as well-known as Ap Chundu, but he is also a protective deity and is believed to have a yak's head.

At one time Ap Joyak was very powerful. One day he decided to take a trip south to India, and soon after arriving there he saw a young woman, Ache Gyem. Her father was a demon and her mother a goddess, but Ap Joyak didn't know this. He just knew that she was beautiful—thin and tall and full of grace. He could not keep his eyes off her.

As it turns out, part of his fascination with Ache Gyem might have been due to the fact that they had been soul mates in their previous incarnations. Whatever the reason, he fell madly in love with her and decided to bring her to Haa as his wife. Vowing to do so, but leaving his beloved Ache Gyem behind, Ap Joyak made his return to Haa. Now, back in Haa there was an official leader, Luni Tshering Dorji, who served him. Ap Joyak knew how loyal Luni Tshering Dorji was to him, and so he sent him to India to fetch the beautiful Ache Gyem. Luni Tshering Dorji dutifully took the long trip south to India and in due course he did indeed find Ache Gyem. But her beauty was so great that when he arrived at her home and saw her, Luni Tshering Dorji also immediately fell in love with her.

Now the scales tipped and lust for Ache Gyem outweighed his loyalty to Ap Joyak. Instead of bringing her to Ap Joyak, he brought her as far as Haa Jangkana, the southernmost part of Haa valley. He kept her there as his wife, and Ache Gyem eventually became pregnant with his child. But he wasn't a good husband to her. He beat her regularly even once she had become pregnant. When it was time to eat, he neglected her, just giving her the bones from his meat. The lack of food and her regular punishments took their toll, and eventually Ache Gyem's celestial beauty disappeared.

All this time Luni Tshering Dorji was very afraid that Ap Joyak would find out about his wicked act. Finally, it distressed him so much that he decided to try to send Ache Gyem along with her baby back to India. But prophecy is a powerful thing: because Ap Joyak and Ache Gyem were prophesied to be soul mates, once she started to walk down the road toward India with her baby on her back, she somehow became turned around and headed directly for the home of Ap Joyak. She reached the shore of a lake just above Haa Jangkana, where Luni Tshering Dorji's home was. He saw her and understanding that she was heading toward Ap Joyak, he shot her with an arrow. She died in an instant, falling into the lake with the baby on her back. Today that lake is considered to be Ache Gyem's soul lake, Jakam told me.

Even today, she said, you can see the beautiful cloth with which Ache Gyem tied her baby to her back. Because of this tragedy and betrayal of Ap Joyak, the people of Haa have to go to the soul lake and make offerings to Ache Gyem once a year. Ache Gyem continues to be available to the people of Haa through the nyenjom for whom she is a tutelary deity.

After telling the story of her deity to Chencho and me, Jakam explained how she makes her divinations. She had two techniques, she explained: with dice and with rice. When she uses dice, the person who is consulting her has to hold the dice first, make a wish, and then roll them. When she sees the numbers, she divines whether they are good or bad. When sick people come to visit, she uses rice for divination.

The sick person gives rice to the nyenjom, then the nyenjom throws it to find out what's wrong. The pattern of the rice on the floor determines which ritual the sick person must perform, including an offering of ritual cakes, or *torma*, at home. If the person is an alcoholic you have to offer alcohol, she said. But in some cases, she just prescribes home remedies. She pointed out that sometimes people will suspect that a dead person is causing the sickness, but if that is indeed the problem, she won't reveal the dead person's name. She explained that when she is praying, her tutelary deity, Ache Gyem, goes into the back of her head; when the words come out of her mouth when she is praying, it's not her, Jakam, who is speaking—it's Ache Gyem. She said that sometimes the mind of a deceased person goes inside her mind and gives her all kinds of information about those who are suffering.

Besides her own tutelary deity, Jakam explained, there was a broad range of deities that inhabit the Haa valley, whose own lives were completely intertwined with the lives of the people who were settled in the valley.

I think it was while she was recounting this next story that it dawned on me how I had completely misjudged my capacity to understand other people's experiences. Or perhaps there are points along the way in life when you suddenly wake up and realize that not everyone sees the world exactly as you do, and this was one of those moments: the world outside the little house where we were sitting, with the light coming through the small opening that served as a window. By now the cat had moved to bathe in the sunbeams. As she talked with obvious clarity and certainty about what she was saying, telling us the founding story of her village in Haa, I realized that I did not see the half of what was in front of me, which was completely clear and available to her. And here is the story she told us.

Once there was an astrologer named Gyep Donge Tsip, who was also the lord of that region. In that region there were also two spirits who together were called Chubja Do Dum, which essentially means the deities of rock. These demons gave birth to a baby boy, whose name was Chana Dorji. The two demons were very jealous of Gyep Donge Tsip. They wanted nothing more than to take his place and become the rulers over the region.

The Chubja Do Dum started to do whatever they could to cause harm to the region, but Gyep Donge Tsip kept foiling their attempts to cause damage. Finally, the two demons made a terrible plan. They abandoned their son, Chana Dorji, in front of Gyep Donge Tsip's palace and sneaked inside. Once inside the palace, they transformed all the servants into blacksmiths and other kinds of people who were from a lower class and therefore very impure. They knew that Gyep Donge Tsip himself was kind and pure, pure enough to be able to practice astrology and do the work of a medium. It is said that he was the very first pawo, or male nyenjom. Because of his purity, the demons knew that these impure people would definitely affect his health and make him ill. And so it happened that because of all the contamination, Gyep Donge Tsip suffered a great deal and eventually even contracted leprosy.

In the meantime, after the Chubja Do Dum had abandoned Chana Dorji at the doorstep while they enacted their evil plan, the astrologer had found the child and adopted him, raising him as his own son with great kindness. By the time Chana Dorji was nine years old, he began searching for a nyenjom who could cure his adoptive father. He searched everywhere for a cure. At some point someone told him that there were two spirits who had the power of a nyenjom, and so he should seek them out—perhaps they could cure his father. Not knowing that the spirits he was told about were his parents, he followed the directions he was given, which led him to the place where the Chubja Do Dum lived. He told the entire story to the two demons and they promised to do a ritual. But of course, the ritual they performed was not real. They had no intention of curing the one whom they were hoping to someday replace.

That night after the ritual, Chana Dorji had a dream in which he saw the Chubja Do Dum, and immediately he understood that they were in fact his parents. Soon thereafter, Gyep Donge Tsip did indeed pass away. But before that Gyep Donge Tsip had already prayed and asked the gods, the deities, and his spiritual teacher that after his death they send another medium to the world for the well-being of sentient beings.

Chana Dorji, the adopted son of Gyep Donge Tsip, was very angry. He knew the demons, his own parents, had killed his father. He took his bow and arrow and went to kill them. Finally he found them, but the Chubja Do Dum transformed into insects and hid under the rocks of the courtyard.

Chana Dorji didn't consider himself defeated. Although his name is Vajrapani, the Buddhist deity, in this story he is in fact an emanation of Guru Rinpoche. He started meditating, making offerings and prayers. He asked for help from the protective deities and nagas, or water spirits, known as *lu* in Bhutan. Soon, with the help of the protectors, a thunderbolt came from the sky; with the help of the lu, water flowed all over the ground. Finally, the rocks cracked, water flowed everywhere, into every crack and crevice, and the Chubja Do Dum, who were then in insect form, were drowned and thus subdued.

As Gyep Donge Tsip had wished, the gods sent a bird to be a nyenjom. When the bird came to earth, she took on the responsibilities of a nyenjom, but in fact, because of her divine origin she was actually a khandrom.

It dawned on me that the story of this bird was actually her personal story. The nyenjom who had invited me into her house was the reincarnation of the original nyenjom, sent to Haa in the form of a bird. Here she sits before me, Jakam, White Bird, a wrinkled old woman with twisted feet. As I write this now, I know that, but at the time, I was captivated, hanging on to the details of an elaborate and beautiful fairy tale.

When the bird turned into a nyenjom, she didn't have a house, so she prayed to the gods for one. The gods sent down a divine carpenter named Tulku Zowa Baley to build a house for her. The house that the carpenter built was strong, beautiful, and warm. So, after the house was finished, naturally all her neighbors wanted a house just like hers. Tulku Zowa Baley agreed to build all her neighbors houses as well. Not only did the village grow into a place of beautifully built houses; the nyenjom became very popular in the village and many visitors came to her for divinations. But because of the visitors' pollution and contamination, the nyenjom got sick and ended up with leprosy.

Now, there was another nyenjom in the area whose name was Janna Au Tse Gem. She told the neighbors to get the nyenjom with leprosy out of the village. She said that the nyenjom and her clothes should be taken to India for the safety of the people so that they wouldn't also contract leprosy. The villagers took the nyenjom to India and hung her on a tree. She was so severely ill while hanging in the tree that she could only move her thumb. She prayed to the gods for protection. In truth, the second nyenjom hoped to depose the sick nyenjom, who, as it turns out, was a khandrom of divine origin. After a few days the sick nyenjom received a letter from her divine father and mother. It fell onto her arm, and she read it with her thumb. The letter said they would send five khandroms to perform a ritual to cure her leprosy. Soon the five khandroms arrived.

In order to perform the ritual, the five khandroms needed five pure girls, as well as offerings of milk, butter, meat, and alcohol. The five khandroms found almost everything that they needed except for a crown, a hand drum, and a bell. To find this they traveled to each place where the five pure girls lived, four of whom lived in each of the four directions. The youngest one lived in Paro, at the center of the four directions. The pure girl who came from the eastern part of Bhutan was called Sha Dorji Rigi Khandrom, and she had the crown, bell, and drum. But now they needed a key.

They traveled to visit the pure girl in the south, because she was supposed to have the key. Her name was Lho Rinchen Sege Khandrom, but as it turns out, she didn't have the key, so they went to the young pure girl in the west. Her name was Nup Pema Rigi

Khandrom. But as it turned out, she also didn't have the key. So Nup Pema Rigi Khandrom sent the khandroms on their way and they headed to the north. There they met Jang Yeshey Khandrom. But even there in the north there was no key.

The pure village girl at the center was named Ue Bidha Rigi Khandrom. She was still in Paro, and so after searching all four directions the khandroms finally returned to Paro to see her. Sure enough, when they reached the village they found the key and all the instruments they needed. Once they had finally collected the crown, the hand bell, the drum, and the key, they started performing rituals for the suffering nyenjom who was still in India tied to the tree. As soon as the rituals were performed, the nyenjom was instantly cured of her leprosy. She transformed back into a bird and flew into the sky and back to her divine parents.

From that time forward, she explained, nyenjoms have existed in the world. In western Bhutan it is believed that an emanation of the khandrom is given the title of nyenjom. Today each household in all parts of western Bhutan—Haa, Paro, Punakha, Wangdue Phodrang, and Gasa—makes an offering and performs a ritual. A nyenjom is invited to make offerings every year in each house in the village.

When she finished her story, we sat in silence for a few minutes. The cat woke up and made her way to the doorway, predicting the end of our gathering. Pema Dema, our hostess, started to talk with her friend Jakam. Their conversation washed over me, untranslated, which was fine. I had a lot to sort out, and it was nice to just sit for a moment to allow it all to settle in. As their talking wound down, the afternoon was turning into early evening, and we still had to get Pema Dema back to her house and ourselves back to Thimphu. We said our goodbyes and clambered back into the van. Leaving Pema Dema at her house, we waved goodbye to her and her family, and the van rumbled along the narrow dirt road, slowly climbing along the steep valley walls, out of this narrow sliver of life and land called Haa, and up to the Chelela pass, which at almost 13,000 feet is one of the highest passes in Bhutan. There we stopped for a few minutes watching nuns in maroon robes carrying heavy loads of firewood on their backs to a nunnery that we could spot maybe a mile down a long path from the main road. We got out of the van to breathe, to take in this wide expanse of sky and almost nothing else besides prayer flags fluttering along the pass, though I could almost not catch any breath at all at that high and lonely spot.

8

THE STORY OF A FATHER AND
HIS RIZAM DAUGHTER

Whenever we were driving, my guide Chencho was constantly talking or texting with friends, friends of friends, or someone else's uncle, tracking down where the next rizam, nyenjom, and khandrom might be, and which ones might be willing to meet us. The same night that we returned to Thimphu, Chencho found out about another rizam whom people were also calling "khandrom." He was told that she lived in an area between Paro and Haa called Dawakha, and so Françoise, Chencho, and I made a plan to go visit her at her house, high on a ridge, the following morning.

Early morning in Thimphu is quiet. There's the sound of ravens calling in the trees and far across the valley. A few cars and trucks pass by and I hear the sound of someone out on the street sweeping yesterday's dust. A profusion of lavender wisteria flowers hangs from the vines that climb the walls of the guesthouse, and the willow trees are leafed out in an abundance of pale spring green. The softness of spring here is not at all what I had envisioned spring in these high mountains to be like.

All of us converged at the van. Françoise had her thermos of tea and a basket of cookies, and every other necessary thing she might fit into her satchel, and we climb in and start the drive out of Thimphu heading west.

The house was a traditional Bhutanese farmhouse with white-washed walls and a timbered frame, flowers and sacred symbols painted on all four sides, and the timbers also emblazoned with floral motifs. The front wall of the house was painted with two deer, a buck on one side of the door and a doe on the other. On one side a clothesline was strung up the length of the house. A bucket of laundry was soaking in the sun as was a dog, typically black with brown eyebrows. The view from the back of the house was into an apple orchard and past it, farther out across the valley and the woods beyond. A couch, excavated at some earlier date for its cushioning, could have still potentially been used as a place to take in this view.

Walking inside, the smooth dark wood planks of the floor were polished to a shine by generations of feet wearing them down. Inside the house the small rooms were painted all over with hand stenciled designs. We arrived as two other women had just walked in the doorway. A young woman ushered all of us into a room where yet another woman was waiting. Clearly the woman we had come to meet was popular. Françoise started to chat with the other women there with us, and we learned that the two women who arrived ahead of us were of Nepali descent, living in Paro. They told us that they had come all the way to Dawakha because there was no other khandrom in Paro. "Khandrom" is what they called her.

One of the young women taught at the hospitality and tourism school in Paro. Her husband was dead and she was raising two girls by herself, hoping to get a job in Australia. The other was a tailor who also worked in Paro. While Françoise chatted with them, Chencho disappeared down the hallway.

Françoise and I were then escorted into the room where the rizam was sitting and where we were eventually joined by Chencho. The focal point of the room was a raised wooden platform where the rizam sat in a cloud of incense that emanated from three different incense burners to protect her from impurities. When I first entered the room, the smoke was so thick I could barely see, much less breathe, but after a while the smoke dissipated some, and it all became more tolerable.

The rizam's niece was in the room along with us as her attendant. She helped to light the incense when it burned out, but I also think she was keeping an eye on us Westerners to make sure we didn't try anything, like taking a photo, which, she told Chencho, was not okay.

The rizam quickly straightened us out concerning the use of the word *khandrom* and told us plainly that she was not one. Chencho plugged away with questions about her experience of the hells: did she actually die and go to the hells? She didn't seem to think so.

The rizam was interrupted at unpredictable moments by some kind of possession that made her stomach growl in the most profound way. The duration of our visit with her was only an hour, but in the course of that time she made it clear she was happy to speak with us and was especially happy that we were interested in the hells. People these days don't have much interest in the hells anymore, she said. She wished that they did.

In our conversation, she told us that the first khandrom was Jigme Choezom. In those ancient times, she said, there was no reincarnation. Ngawang Pelzom was the first reincarnation of Jigme Choezom, and today she was the third generation. She told us she makes offerings and meditates on the goddess Tara as her deity and prays to her to alleviate the suffering of all beings. Through divination and offering to the protective local deities—Ap Chundu, Ache Gyem, and Tsheringma—she helps the suffering beings all over the country, whether they are rich or poor, but mostly she is helping the poor people, she says.

She told us that she had been to the eighteen hells but couldn't say much more than that. It's difficult to categorize what type of shaman she is given the choices we have. Is she a delom? Not really. A nyenjom? I suppose in some way, but it seems like she's more interested in teaching and advising people about the hell realms than in the fortune-telling kind of divination that she is regularly called upon to do. But why exactly do we need to categorize her anyhow?

As we finally left, once again we were told "no photos" and headed next door to the miniscule room at the front of the neighbor's house that serves as the local shop. It was smoky from the fire in the wood-burning stove, but it was warm and smelled delicious. There was a television turned on to the National Geographic channel. Some local workmen on a tea break were watching with rapt attention as orca whales splashed through a turquoise ocean. The smell must have been from the pakoras, an Indian snack made from chickpea flour, vegetables, oil, salt, and spices. We dug right in.

While we ate, Chencho told us that while we were in the waiting room with the other two women, he was in the kitchen chatting with the rizam's eighty-three-year-old father, Ap Tashi, who told him the story of Yeshey Choden, his daughter whom we had just met. She called herself "rizam," but according to her father, Yeshey Choden is a true delom. She learned everything with her previous khandrom incarnation's help and support, he said. Her signs came when she was thirteen years old.

Yeshey Choden was educated up to the fourth grade, he told Chencho. She was an intelligent and hardworking student. Then her elder sister gave birth and the family stopped her schooling so that Yeshey could look after her sister's baby. She then helped with the baby and the farmwork until she started to suffer from an unknown illness.

When she was sick, the nyenjom from Haa, Aum Jakam, came and did divinations, but that didn't help her. She continued to suffer from madness, so Yeshey Choden's father and mother brought her to the hospital. Over the years she received numerous injections and medicine from the hospital, but none of that helped either.

At some point, Ap Tashi and the family thought their daughter's sickness could not be cured. Finally, they decided to visit another nyenjom, although they had already visited many mediums. They had heard about a Tibetan couple. The woman did divinations, while the man worked as a caretaker for an orchard. When the Tibetan nyenjom performed a divination, she discovered that Yeshey Choden was indeed an incarnation of a deity. Finally, she concluded that their daughter was the reincarnation of none other than Ache Gyem, whose cloth is still seen in the lake. They were told to go home and prepare alcohol to bring as an offering to Ache Gyem in Haa.

They prepared the alcohol and traveled to a holy lake in Haa dedicated to Ache Gyem. There they made offerings and performed rituals, and Yeshey Choden also meditated. But still her health did not improve. Ap Tashi said they did many rituals to different deities and Yeshey Choden practiced many types of meditation as she was instructed to do, but she still didn't find her deity and her ill health continued.

They brought many monks and masters to their home to perform rituals, but nothing seemed to helped her. People in their village started speculating that she was now in her last stage of life and was going to die. The family was close to giving up hope.

But Ap Tashi wasn't ready to give up on his daughter. He decided to take Yeshey Choden back to Aum Jakam. That evening Jakam started preparing for the ritual and divination. The father said he was very nervous of course, but Jakam told him, "Don't worry. Whatever it is, the result will come today."

To do the ritual and divination many objects needed to be obtained: nine different kinds of stone, nine different kinds of jewels, nine different kinds of tree, and even new clothes. Finally, everything was ready and Aum Jakam started the ritual. During the ritual, Ap Tashi recounted to us, Aum Jakam said that a khandrom, Meto Saday from the Shar Wangdue Phodrang region, was her previous incarnation. She also said that Meto Saday would show her the way and teach her divination and other rituals.

A few minutes after the ritual began, Aum Jakam tried to give Yeshe Choden the rizam crown, thereby making her a rizam. But then Khandrom Meto Saday took possession of Yeshey Choden and said, "Aum Jakam, you are my student. Who are you to give me a crown and recognize me?" And then, said Ap Tashi, Yeshey Choden put the crown on herself.

From that time on, Yeshey Choden, the Dawakha rizam, visited Meto Saday's home village every year to make offerings and perform rituals. After Aum Jakam recognized Meto Saday to be his daughter's previous incarnation, said Ap Tashi, she was cured from her sickness. And that's when she began to do divination as her main work.

Usually, local rizams only work with one deity, but it gets a little complicated, because in Yeshey Choden's case, she has not one but three deities who possess her. Meto Saday is her main deity, but Meto Saday is also the previous incarnation of Aum Jakam. So Yeshey Choden is able to be possessed by Meto Saday as well as the nyenjom Jakam's deities. Basically, she is available to whichever deity comes first, and she has to worship equally all deities she is connected with.

After the ritual, Aum Jakam advised the family to appoint a spiritual teacher for their daughter. They traveled to Thimphu to meet with the lama Samtrel Rinpoche. After he agreed to be Yeshey Choden's spiritual teacher and he performed all the necessary rituals, Yeshey Choden started feeling better overall. That relief lasted for some time, but after a year she once again started feeling unwell. Nevertheless, as long as she was practicing meditation she managed to stay reasonably well. Her mantras were very clear. She has now been doing divination and rituals as well as meditation for the suffering beings for more than thirty years.

Ap Tashi continued by saying that to be able to do divinations, his daughter also needed to be taught by an astrologer so she could receive instruction in the practicalities of divinations. She would need to learn how to interpret dice once they were thrown. She also needed to learn how to make divinations by counting rosary beads and rice patterns. After that, she was able to start doing divinations and predictions on her own.

He also mentioned that a few conditions were necessary for making accurate divinations, and once these were achieved, she was able to make divinations without much interference, including being free of environmental or karmic pollution and contamination. She needs to keep clean all the time.

If Yeshey Choden were to go around publicly as the incarnation of Meto Saday, that would mean she could claim rights to the belongings of Meto Saday's family, which are now in their possession in Sha. She didn't want to do that because she would be embarrassed to take the ritual objects that belonged to Meto Saday from her descendants. Instead, she decided to worship Meto Saday without claiming any ownership over her personal belongings. She prayed to Tara, the Buddhist deity of compassion, who is on a much higher plane, and Tara helped her resolve this dilemma.

So now, Chencho concluded, his daughter has achieved greatness as the Dawakha rizam. She now has the authority to perform the rituals that invoke Ache Gyem, Ap Chundu, and Meto Saday, as well as those of Tsheringma, the Buddhist deity of long life who resides on the Jomolhari mountain north of Paro and Haa.

After we drink up our butter tea Françoise buys some extra pakoras to bring home, and we head back out to the van. That night back in my hotel room I write up my notes until I can't write anymore, then read from academic tomes on Buddhism and on shamanism, trying to make sense of the account we were told. Eventually, when my brain gives up trying to load in new information, I wander the streets of Thimphu aimlessly, staring through shop windows, my mind a complete deadweight.

Wanting to break free from the town and my head entirely, I put on my running shoes and run the several miles along the road that leads uphill, out of town, to the shining Golden Buddha statue. There he sits on his golden throne at the end of 108 steps, a recently completed work of glamor that is now a focal point for the skyline of Thimphu. Walking inside the temple that is housed underneath, the gold walls amplify the whispers of the devotees and other tourists, and I am calmed by the immensity of the room and of the possibilities that Buddha's vision of reality has offered. When I return, Françoise suggests another interview, but she is busy so this time it's just Chencho and me who head out in the van to search out the next rizam.

9

The Rizam of the Monastery

Neyphug monastery's full name is Thegchen Choling, or, more to the point, Dharma Land of Vajrayana. Located far up the side of a steep ravine on the eastern slopes of the Paro valley, it sits above the expanse of rice paddies broken into pieces by stretches of forest on the valley floor below. The tulku of the monastery lives there part of the time with his mother, who calls herself Ani Rizam. *Ani* means "nun," and *rizam* means, well, "rizam." Ani Rizam is a rizam, a nun, and a delom. On this spot, and within her, the revered world of the monastery and the world of the divine messengers, normally on the periphery, meet in a headlong collision.

I awoke early in the morning on the day that Chencho and I were heading out to find her. My guesthouse room was still dark and cold. The sun had not yet come over the trees into the Thimphu valley. I made tea from the kettle and began to read.

As the story goes, Guru Padmasambhava first arrived in Bhutan during the eighth century. Soon after, he traveled from valley to valley, across every pass and mountaintop, every river and stream. Along the way he encountered local deities everywhere he went, and so, as he went, he tamed each and every one of them, and each and every one of them became a guardian of Buddhism. As he traveled, he sometimes also left imprints of his hands and feet on the faces of rocks throughout the countryside. In the process he hid sacred objects—objects that preserved teachings, sacred vows, and other precious things in certain places, including in the very location where the Neyphug monastery was founded by the treasure discoverer Ngawang Drakpa in the sixteenth century. And so, the spot began to be called Neyphug, meaning the sacred hermitage cave. The local pronunciation is "Heyphug," so it is also called the Heyphug Monastery. If you were to walk for about an hour due south of the monastery you would reach the stupa that contains the relics of Mahakasayapa, one of the principal disciples of the Buddha. The devotees of the monastery say that these relics make this stupa one of the holiest stupas throughout the Himalayas.

Walking about one hour in the other direction leads to another stupa, called the Self-Arisen Stone Stupa, or Do Chorten, which has great spiritual value for pilgrims. Clearly this is a significant monastery to the Bhutanese. It is well known in the pilgrimage circuit of Paro, even though you won't find it in any guidebook.

As the springtime sun finally began to warm the valley, Chencho arrived to pick me up. By now Chencho had become pretty adept at taking the lead in all our conversations. We were a team now, and I had gotten comfortable with him asking all our key questions without having to translate back to English in between.

The air was fine with early morning mist, muting the colors to shades of gray, making sounds too quiet, and obscuring the view of the hills around us as we trundled out of Thimphu. Soon the mist cleared to reveal a paved blacktop road ahead of the van, heading through the wide, fertile Paro valley. At this altitude and this early in spring, planted fields were still fallow, waiting for a deepening of the season to turn over to full verdant green.

Once we were further northeast into the valley, we turned off the pavement onto a dirt road, clearly well-used and wide enough for two cars to pass, that traced a line along a riverbed that led away from the town, from the center of the valley, toward the steep hills beyond. The river was low, rushing over pebbles and rocks, as clear as glass, as it meandered down from the hills through the rice paddies. Low cut rice straw drew a checkerboard pattern, left from last year's harvest. At first, as we cut further through the fields heading toward the valley walls, plenty of smaller, single-track farm roads and walking paths joined up with this larger road, the way little streams add up, engorging a larger river as you head upstream. And, like a river narrows closer to the headwaters, as we headed further into the valley the extra tracks thinned out and the road diminished. As we passed by the last farm of the valley, the road was only wide enough for one car at best. We followed it, now essentially a generous pony path, as it wound up switchbacks carved into the side of the mountain.

At this point Chencho and I had traveled together through passes so high that I could hardly breathe, along roads so narrow that they can really only be described as glorified footpaths, and along dry riverbeds that are obviously roads only when it's not pouring rain. By now I was accustomed to all kinds of roads and road variants in Bhutan. Nevertheless.

This road was steep and narrow and windy like something out of a storybook, when the prince is on his way to find the ogre who he must deceive in order to find the princess hidden in the deep recesses of the castle and make a harrowing rescue and escape. If that could describe a quality of a road, then it was this one.

But instead of a castle inhabited by an ogre and an imprisoned princess, at the end of this road was a monastery inhabited by maroon-robed monks, their tulku, and the tulku's mother. The road leveled out just before it reached this spot, here on the face of the mountain. The monastery was surrounded by trees, its old walls were painted with the traditional whitewash. But mostly it was soft and brown, like the ground it was built on, and like the color of the stone where new walls were being built to replace ones that had fallen in an earthquake the year before. A wall of about hip height ran along the length of the driveway, creating a perfect perch, if you're a bird or a tired traveler, for looking out over the wide expanse of the deep black shade of evergreen forest and beyond, the narrow valley below; the arching luminous blue sky high above.

Chencho and I looked out long enough to catch our breath, and only a minute passed before a young monk was sent to fetch us and find out what we were doing here. Chencho told the boy that we had come to meet Ani Rizam, and we were brought through the massive brown mud walls by way of an open doorway that led into a hallway and invited to sit in a room with shiny red couches made brighter by electric lights.

Chencho's introduction of who we were and the purpose of our visit apparently seemed slightly suspicious to the monks who greeted us, because a long discussion ensued in the hallway outside the room where we were waiting, but eventually the conversation died down and they left us to our own devices. We waited on the red couches for what seemed like hours.

Ani Rizam finally appeared in the doorway. I recall her as unusually tall, although it could be that I remember her that way because she had that kind of powerful presence, that aura some people have that makes you think of them as being larger than they are. Her long black hair was pulled back into a bun, and she wore long maroon robes with a wide smile and large inquisitive eyes. She invited us to kindly have some tea with her, and soon the same young monks who had given us suspicious glares were now ordered to pour us milk tea and serve us biscuits.

Chencho told her in a nutshell the reason for our visit and immediately she responded that she was thrilled to hear that we were researching the deloms, rizams, and nyenjoms of Bhutan, proclaiming, essentially, that it's about time these important spiritual figures got the recognition they deserve. Your research will help all sentient beings, she said. She launched right into her own story.

She told us that her given name was Yeshey Choden. It's pretty common in Bhutan to have similar names, so I wasn't too surprised that she shared a name with the rizam we had just met. She was sixty-five years old and the mother of the Neyphug tulku, the reincarnated lama and spiritual leader of this monastery.

Her son, the Neyphug Tulku Sherdrup Chokyi Nyima, was born in Paro in 1980 to Yeshey and her husband, Tsultrim Tharchin. She said the signs were there from the beginning that her son was not going to be an ordinary boy. Some of what I found written about the monastery in the tulku's biography on their website before our drive had to do with her and her son, his magical conception, and the signs foretelling his role:

> When his mother conceived him, she had many dreams and saw signs that foretold about the birth of an extraordinary child. One month after his conception, his mother dreamt a crystal pillar as high as the sky with a white sheep and a small bronze vessel filled with milk next to it. She then held the sheep and sprinkled the milk as an offering. Again, after two months, she dreamt of dribbling nectar above Neyphug monastery. At the same time, all the people of Do Chorten, near Neyphug, saw one end of the rainbow fall over his mother's house while the other end fell on the monastery.[8]

After the rainbow appeared, a tree that grew just below the house bloomed for a second time. Everything was adding up to an accumulation of signs of a special birth. Then one day Yeshey was walking along the Panglog pass, which leads to the sacred place of Do Chorten, when she heard thunder in the clouds that hovered low in the sky. She looked up and saw what appeared to be two nuns walking ahead of her. Once she reached the spot where they had been standing, they turned into two balls of radiant light emanating five colors, that then turned into two crystals at her feet on the road where she walked. Naturally she did what anyone would do: she picked up the crystals and put them in her pocket. The crystals were later used as *dharana*—amulets with special powers—that are inserted into statues of deities to imbue them with the reminder of virtue. Finally, when Yeshey was about to give birth, she had a dream of two rising suns over the horizon and the blowing of a white conch, which was mounted on a throne.

Eventually her son was recognized as the current ninth reincarnation, or tulku, of Neyphug and later became the spiritual head of the monastery. Once all this was explained, Ani began to describe her own life, which has been equally full of mysterious signs leading to an extraordinary path.

"I was born here in Paro," she told us. "Both my parents were
farmers. When I was young there were many signs." Three-year-old
Yeshey's favorite game was to perform pretend spiritual rituals. But
while she was still just three years old, her mother fell ill.

"When I turned three, my mother started acting insane. Many
times, my family tried to perform spiritual rituals and visited a
nyenjom to make my mother well." But nothing worked. During
that time her family suffered a lot. Around fourteen of their cows
and oxen died without any apparent signs of sickness. Yeshey did
rituals for the animals, making all kinds of offering cakes out of
flour, called *torma*, for the local deities. Her mother was suffering,
and the animals were dying—her family was truly at a loss about
what to do in this terrible situation.

They heard that in Tibet there was a very great lama called Samdrup Choling Rinpoche, so they decided to walk from Paro to
Tibet to meet this lama and see if he might be able to help Yeshey's
mother. When they arrived, Rinpoche performed many rituals,
but none seemed to help much. Her mother was still suffering
greatly. The lama pondered and looked through his religious texts.
Finally he declared, "It is because of your daughter. Your daughter
is a very powerful deity from the place where three mountains and
three rivers come together," a place called Sha Gulikha. "You will
be healed after your daughter begins to talk. Your daughter is a
reincarnation of a delom." The family thanked the rinpoche, gathered their belongings, and began the long walk back home to Paro.

Ten years later, when Yeshey turned thirteen, she started doing
divinations and making predictions, until one day she walked into
the main room of the house where her parents were sitting and
announced, "I am Namgay Choezom from Sha. Why am I here at
Aum Sangay Zam (her mother's) house?" They realized then and
there that Yeshey was indeed the reincarnation of Namgay Choezom, who had been a famous delom many generations before.

When someone has the realization of being a reincarnation, it's customary to make a pilgrimage to the former incarnation's village in order to better connect with their emanation and their living descendants. So Yeshey decided to go visit Sha Gulikha, the home of Namgay Choezom. Back then there was no road, and so she and her family walked. And it was at that point when she made her first visit to Sha Gulikha, she explained, that she first died and traveled to the hells. The prophecy of her previous incarnation stated that she would have to visit the hell realms several times. She visited the hell realms again, for three days, when she was staying at Menchuna in the Punakha valley, and then again when she was staying at Phajoding in the Thimphu valley, also for three days.

Thinking back on it all, she said to us, it would be helpful if people could light butter lamps and recite mantras when rizams are in the hell realms, because it makes it easier to stay there for a longer time. She explained that if people who are near the body of the rizam make a lot of chatter while she is in the hell realms it disturbs her and can force her to come back to her body.

After explaining this to Chencho and me, she considered this point for a minute; perhaps that was another reason why she might have needed to make several visits to the hell realms: when rizams are disturbed by noise and pollution, it makes them leave the hell realms prematurely. But then again, even when they have completed visiting all eighteen hells, some still need to return in order to fulfill their prophecy, she said.

One of the young monks came back into the room where we were sitting, refilling our cups of milk tea and glancing sideways at Chencho and me, clearly curious about who we might be. I picked up my cup and took a sip of tea, although at that point I was fairly floating in the stuff. I didn't want Ani Rizam to be distracted in any way from her story, so I kept my eyes on her while I did so as she proceeded to tell us more.

At thirteen years old she was already acting like a rizam, she continued, making predictions concerning everyone she met. Her reputation grew as many visitors started to come to her. Dice was her divination tool when she first started. She didn't have a yidam, a tutelary deity with which she was particularly connected. She didn't understand the Buddhist astrology that was practiced by some of the monks with all the charts. Nevertheless, she firmly believed that her previous incarnation was the delom Namgay Choezom.

In those days, back when she was young, she told us, there was a formal inspection process for women who showed signs of being a rizam to determine whether or not they were authentic. They would be taken to the assembly hall at the Punakha Dzong. The ministers and the chief abbot would be there, and the government officials would inspect her, and finally the Je Khenpo himself, assisted by the monastic body, would question her. In their inspection they would ask questions like: Why are you a rizam? Who was your previous deity? Who was your previous incarnation?

If a woman did not know the identity of her previous deity or if she could not give a reason as to why she was a rizam, then she would be put in jail for three years; the mother of the rizam would be put in jail for twelve years, since making false claims that a girl was a rizam was considered to be a trick primarily instigated by the mother. But today, she said, due to the kindness of the king, there is no longer such a thing as rizam inspections. Anybody could claim to be a rizam these days.

Ani Rizam's story continued to unfold for us. The monastic body led by Je Khenpo and the district administration requested that she come to the assembly at Punakha Dzong. In order to get there, she would have to spend the night at a place called Sa Potala and then cross the Pochu river. Sa Potala was on the hilltop above Changjokha, where today no more than two houses remain. While she was there, many visitors came to her for divinations and predictions. People started talking about her and soon word of her presence reached the ears of government officials.

The government sent some inspectors to meet her en route; in other words, an inspection happened on the way to the inspection. The inspectors, along with some people from the surrounding region, had planned to accompany her until Sha Gulikha. "the Sha rizam, if she is the true reincarnation of Rizam Namgay Choezom, will be able to lead the way," stated one of the officials. Even though this was her first time in the Sha region and she was only thirteen years old, she did in fact lead the way, with the official inspectors and all the people following the path behind her as she walked.

Eventually they reached a place called Rinchengang, opposite Wangdue Phodrang. It was almost dark and they were worried about finding a place to stay, but suddenly a man from Rinchengang came toward her, telling the group, "Oh, my khandrom has come!" The group took that as a sign, and they stopped there for the night.

While they were there, even more visitors came to her for divinations. A man came to her saying that his wife had jumped into the river and they hadn't found her body. He asked for her help in finding her, which she did. The next day as they walked, the group lost their way. Yeshey then saw a dog and realized it was showing the way, so they followed in that direction and, indeed, they reached Sha Gulikha. Yeshey and her cohorts spent three days there—enough time, it was supposed, to determine whether or not she was in fact the true reincarnation of Delom Namgay Choezom.

Now at that time there was a very old woman named Rinchen Dem living in Sha Gulikha. When she was eight years old, she was adopted by none other than the delom, Namgay Choezom, who was already more than eighty years old when she had adopted Rinchen Dem. The people and the government inspectors decided that if Ani Rizam could recognize Rinchen Dem as her daughter, then she was the true reincarnation of Namgay Choezom.

In the morning all the people gathered there. Rinchen Dem came with a bamboo basket with all the things that had belonged to Namgay Choezom.

When she arrived, the young Yeshey slapped the old woman saying, "You have been taken care of by me until now, and only now are you coming here to see me?" After this happened, Yeshey told Rinchen Dem to give her the water container and the statue of the deity Tara, but she didn't need the other things in the basket. At this, the people and government officials who had been crowding around watching all the proceedings consulted together. Finally, the leader of the government officials declared that Yeshey was indeed a true rizam. On she went to her next trial in Punakha Dzong to prove herself to the monks and Je Khenpo.

The Je Khenpo asked her first to explain the meaning of the images in the Wheel of Life, and Yeshey complied. Then he asked her to explain the eighteen hells, and even as a thirteen-year-old girl she was able to do that. Then she was taken inside the assembly hall where they asked her about the thousand buddhas. She didn't answer, but she did point out Avalokiteshvara, the deity of compassion. At that point the monks at Punakha Dzong were convinced of Yeshey's status, performing a ceremony pronouncing that she was the recognized reincarnation of Namgay Choezom.

After she was recognized by the clergy, the government, and the public, the health of her sick mother started to improve. Her mother's mind stabilized and she lived a long and healthy life until her death at eighty-five years old.

After her recognition, the rizam started wearing the maroon robes of a religious person, and she studied Buddhism and meditated in solitude in different caves around Bhutan, visiting many teachers throughout the country. Up until her mid-twenties, people generally referred to her as a nyenjom. But during one of her teachings, she told people to call her "rizam" because she had the power to heal people. It is said that when she went to heal local nyenjoms possessed by unenlightened deities, they became mute and unable to feel their bodies. Some were healed by just her presence.

When she said this, I recalled that nyenjoms, pamos, and pawos also do divination through an unenlightened or mundane deity that possesses them and speaks through them. They are continuously reborn in human form because their role is to make divinations by acting as mediums for an unenlightened or local deity. This stalls their progress toward enlightenment: their continued connection to a mundane deity across lifetimes prevents them from progressing along the path of Buddhism toward a higher realization. It is generally believed that they have to serve the deity until the deity itself becomes enlightened, which won't happen until at least the end of the world. So, they will continue to do divination until then, their enlightenment delayed indefinitely because of their intrinsic value to human beings in the earthly realm.

The delom, on the other hand, according to Ani Rizam, have the spiritual power to stop pamos and nyenjoms from being possessed, freeing them from the endless cycle of acting as mediums and doing divinations, therefore freeing them to progress toward enlightenment. The delom Namgay Choezom was said to have freed five nyenjoms from their roles, after which she gave them all the title of rizam. It was from that time that the villagers began to call these divine messengers *rizam*, and still do so to this day. Namgay Choezom was the one who introduced the term *rizam* in Bhutan centuries ago, according to Yeshey.

For the past fifty years, Yeshey has performed many divinations and many rituals for suffering beings. She also served as a diviner for the royal family of Bhutan. Yeshey told us that she also made a divination in 2003 when Assamese rebels in India set up camps in southern Bhutan as a base to attack India. At that time the fourth king of Bhutan led his army to expel the rebels. Through her divination she saw the king wearing iron clothes protecting him from bullets. She interpreted this as a sign he would win the war. Indeed, the Bhutanese side was successful, and the camps were dismantled.

Despite her recognition, her accurate divinations, and her relationship with the monarchy, Yeshey told us, "Even though I am a rizam, I don't have a proper deity. And even though I am a person, I am uneducated. I am just half a person and half a spirit. Nobody knows what I am, and even I don't know."

Today, although she is still performing divinations, Yeshey said she now has more time to meditate for her own enlightenment and on behalf of suffering beings.

When she finished her story, our tea was long since cold. Yeshey then returned to the nature of our visit. She was so thrilled to have us there at the monastery, she told us. Clearly, she declared, we were sent there by the gods to learn the stories of the deloms and rizams. She hoped our research would bring us all over the country. And she hoped that more and more people would become aware of rizams until the value of all the rizams is recognized throughout the world.

Yeshey, now known more widely as Ani Rizam, ably straddles two worlds, inhabiting both equally: the world of the rizams and their work on behalf of humanity and the world of her son and supporting the monastery. Somehow, by claiming both, she had been accepted by both.

But she sees herself as the exception. She knows that rizams and all divine messengers, all female shamans of the Himalayas, despite being widely relied upon by people from all walks of life in Bhutan, are not openly accepted or even acknowledged. Sometimes their status is outright denied by the same people who patronize them. How many women do work like this, not only lacking acknowledgment, but having their very existence denied because of people's fear of association with something that is not modern or widely accepted through institutional support? That is the life of a rizam in Bhutan. What Ani Rizam was hoping for was simple recognition that divine messengers such as herself truly exist, serve fully in society as who they are, and even play a vital role as spiritual supports for their communites. They deserve to be recognized as such, she said.

Perhaps this recognition is coming. Ani Rizam and the rest have clearly expanded the path of the divine messengers deeper into the Buddhist realm, even into the daily life of some monasteries. Lacking an established lineage to do the work of recognizing their successive reincarnations, they first are recognized primarily by their own communities. Without any formal hierarchy to determine how to name their role in society, they have named themselves: nyenjom, rizam, khandrom, delom.

After talking with Ani Rizam, it becomes clear to me their work is not easy. Their service on behalf of all sentient beings: traversing the hell realms, divining the best course for action in daily life, and generally aligning human needs with the needs of the local deities and the wisdom of the Buddha, all transmitted through their own bodies, often with a huge amount of physical discomfort, is a massive task. But just as clearly, it's a vital strand in the fabric of life in Bhutan.

10

Madness and Retribution

We had been told about another rizam that lived in Punakha, the valley just west of Paro, so bright and early the next day we headed out. Thimphu to Punakha by way of the paved road is about forty-five miles. It threads along the base of the mountains, following the zigzag hem of the narrow valleys and passing through the tiny villages that dot any spot wide enough for the land to flatten out into the shape of a field. Along the roadside, sellers sit with blankets or tarps spread out, waiting patiently for customers, with strings of dried yak cheese and whatever vegetable might be in season at the time. Turning off the blacktop, we followed a smaller dirt road that ended abruptly above a rushing river, white with foam. A steel suspension bridge wide enough to walk on hung high above it, each of its steel cables strung with colored prayer flags—a perfect place for them, I was told, since the constant current of the updrafts created by the rush of water over rocks kept the prayer flags in motion, continuously freeing their prayers into the ether. In a little dirt clearing down by the river, tour guides were preparing inflatable rafts for tourists. It had been such a long drive to get to this seemingly obscure spot that it was a surprise to see people preparing for tourists. It was a surprise to see anyone there, really.

Getting out of the van, we emerged into the little river canyon, nestled deep in the farmland of Punakha. As the bridge swung over the river a hundred feet below, we made our way across. On the other side of the bridge was the path that was walked daily by the people whose farms were on this side of the river. It was also the path to the rizam's house. The pathway there was a walk through a veil of luminous verdant green. Every inch of ground that bordered the fields was crammed with every kind of wild herb and grass. The planted fields were full of every possible crop, but especially rice, all in various stages of budding into the warm, rich air. It was living and breathing green. If there had been any way to bottle that smell, that feeling, for another day, I would have done just that.

As we walked farther from the river, we ventured deeper into the peaceful quiet of a dirt path, of planted earth. A little stream ran down a gully between the terraces, while little birds hopped around the bushes that divided the fields. A hawk sat perfectly still on the branch of a dead tree above the stream, on the lookout for errant fish. Gray skies gave way to rain after awhile, but that abundant springtime of the fields of Punakha made me want to just lie down and wrap myself up in it, sleeping in its warm embrace.

After buying chilis and cucumbers from some of the farmers in their fields, we finally reached the local rizam's house. Climbing the stairs and arriving at her room, the door was closed, but there was a sign out front in Dzongkha clearly stating, "NO PHOTOS, NO RECORDING."

Françoise had visited this rizam earlier in the year, and once we went inside, the rizam recognized her and explained the need for the sign outside the door. Apparently, someone who had visited her had surreptitiously filmed her and then proceeded to post the video on social media without her consent. The rizam explained how dangerous this was because it exposed her to so many impurities, and she had no control whatsoever over what impurities these might be.

Once her explanation was translated back to us I understood the abundance of incense that she and her sister kept lit in front of her at all times. I felt a little apologetic for being there, knowing that, as a foreigner and stranger to the culture, I was also the source of unexpected and uncontrollable impurities. The incense was enough to choke a person, but I hoped for her sake that it was working.

The rizam's name was Phub Zam, and she said she was from

the village Yoebitsa but now she was settled in Nyizergang village, below the magnificent Khamsum Yulley Namgyal Chorten. Phub Zam told us her life story, fraught with suffering and insanity for years and years, before she knew that she was a rizam. When she was young she had a dream in which somebody with the wrathful face of a protector deity took a ritual dagger from her heart and whispered many things to her. When she asked her mother what it could have meant, her family told her it was a sign she was an incarnation of the previous delom, Namgay Choezom. While she was sick, people were talking about her and her madness, saying that perhaps a deity from Japan was inside her mind because previously a Japanese tourist had visited her family's farmhouse. While she was acting mad and suffering, she roamed around the village. During that time the Je Khenpo was conducting a large devotional ceremony at Punakha, which she attended. Je Khenpo was told about Phub Zam and he mentioned she was likely a reincarnation, and so people shouldn't make fun of her. One of the senior monks asked her name, and that's when the "voice from behind her," as she called it, told him that her name was Namgay Choezom, even though her real name was Phub Zam. That was the first time she said to anyone that she was Namgay Choezom. She now considers herself to be a rizam as the reincarnation of the delom Namgay Choezom.

As we were interviewing Phub Zam, she proceeded to provide us with a lineage of the deloms in Bhutan. According to her, the first delom was delom Karma Wangzin; after her there was delom Sangay Choezom, followed by khandrom Pakar Choezom. Her reincarnation was delom Namgay Choezom. After Namgay Choezom was her, Phub Zam. She learned this when the spirit went inside her and spoke, saying "I am Namgay Choezom and I came from Tibet. I suffer because of the previous generation's bad deeds, and so I am here to wash away those sins."

Once Phub Zam had a dream of a woman placing a hat on her head, and when she awoke, her hair was white. When she was asked later whether she had dyed her hair, she replied that her hair had become the same color as Namgay Choezom's had been after she returned from the hells.

She told us that she really wanted to get Namgay Choezom's dagger from her descendants. The ritual dagger had long been a great concern of hers, she explained, because it is said that Namgay Choezom discovered the dagger when she was seventeen years old and was important to the delom. After searching for the dagger, she learned that it had already been bought by a famous tulku who donated it to his monastery as a religious relic, where it is still preserved to this day.

When we told her that we had visited the Paro delom, who is also considered a reincarnation of Namgay Choezom, she became visibly upset. She exclaimed that she had never wanted any controversy. In fact, she had sought out the Paro delom's help, and this is when things went sideways. She said that one day, she unknowingly walked by the place in Paro where the delom lived. When she was in the Paro delom's home, the Paro delom told her to prostrate before her. That's when the voice from the back of her head spoke up, pronouncing through her mouth, "Why should I prostrate before you when I'm as powerful as you are?" Her answer apparently upset the Paro delom, and since then they have had no contact.

When word got around that Phub Zam was the reincarnation of Namgay Choezom, people started to seek her out, coming to her with offerings. According to Phub Zam, this angered the Paro delom even more. She told us she hoped that the two of them could eventually work together, regardless of who held greater authority. She had tried to apologize for saying those things, she said, but the Paro delom would not accept her apology.

Phub Zam, known widely as the Punakha rizam, said she has nothing against the Paro delom. She hadn't meant to say that the Paro delom is not a delom, she told us. In fact she is a delom, she said, but not from Namgay Choezom's lineage. But, she said, she didn't harbor any bad feelings toward her.

Although the Punakha rizam has tried many times to approach

her, the Paro delom would refuse to meet with her. As this controversy unfolded over weeks and months, Phub Zam was dealing with her ongoing bouts of illness as best as she could manage. She was thinking of moving, or perhaps just traveling to Sha Gulikha to be among the descendants of Namgay Choezom. She'd like to go back to Sha Gulikha to have a chance to cement a better bond with her deities, she told us. But generally, she seemed worn out from the physical suffering she endures. One time, she told us, the voice from behind her said, "You will suffer like Namgay Choezom." The life of a rizam on earth is very short, she said, so she doesn't want to waste it. Because of her physical suffering, she lives in a constant dream state, she explained, partly on Earth, partly not.

Our visit with the Punakha rizam was long, and she talked almost without stopping for perhaps an hour, finally interrupted by a kind of seizure. She began to talk with a different voice, and her stomach growled deeply. Her sister looked a little panicked and went to get their father to help. He came into the room where we all sat watching her, none of us knowing what to do. At that point we decided it was probably best for us to give her a chance to rest. She was clearly exhausted from her trances and seizures, all of which are knotted together into what is now her daily life and work. We began to make our way out the door, but as we descended the steps there was already another group of people at the bottom who had just arrived waiting to see her. As we walked back down the path through the fields toward the car, we passed more.

On the walk back to the car Françoise and I discussed our visit with Phub Zam. We had begun to realize that these interviews were drawing us into a deeper story of the divine messengers' role between Buddhism and the shamanic realm in Bhutan, which was clearly alive, well, and perhaps even more central than it ever was. That is not at all what we expected to uncover.

In the space of time that we were visiting the rizam, the tour company had finished getting their boats ready. When we crossed the bridge back to the other side of the river, they were friendly but still had no customers, so they offered us sodas. We all gratefully accepted them. Somehow the gesture just felt like some kind of return to reality. We drove back to Thimphu, our heads filled with what we had heard that day.

I knew that after this interview, my departure from Bhutan was drawing near. We were all getting weary of van trips. As an American and not well-schooled in Buddhism, I struggled daily to comprehend what was going on. Françoise had endless patience with my loads of questions attempting to get a grasp of things, and Chencho faithfully helped interpret everything I witnessed. The entire trip became a group effort of translation of multiple languages and multiple cultures and multiple social obligations and expectations. It was tiring, but we were elated, knowing that we were getting closer to some understanding of the complex and extraordinary world of the divine messengers of Bhutan.

11

Return to Paro

I had just enough time left for one more visit, and so Françoise, Chencho, and I headed back to Paro to search out the khandrom we had met years before. Back at her house, she remembered us immediately despite the many years that had passed. We asked her if she knew about the rizam we had met in Punakha. She immediately dismissed her out of hand. "Many people say that they're a rizam," she pointed out. She cannot say whether they are or not. In fact, she had heard that this Punakha rizam said she is a reincarnation of Namgay Choezom.

According to her, many women claim they are a khandrom, or delom, or rizam, but they are not telling the truth. She considers herself as the authority because of her recognition, and because of her meditation practices, and that by looking at someone's face she can see through them and subdue them.

She told us that when "fake" khandroms come to her house thinking that they're real, the minute they enter her house, she utters a mantra and does the sacred gesture of subjugation. When she does this, the fake khandroms collapse immediately. They then return to their senses and acknowledge that she is the real khandrom.

A khandrom is like a tulku, she explained: in the same way that tulkus are reincarnations of previous lamas, she is a reincarnation of a previous khandrom and so uses her past incarnation's prayers.

This competition between the Punakha rizam and the Paro khandrom might have an economic side, as more power attracts more devotees and offerings, but it's not so simple as all that. This is also about having a genuine role in society. Each of them are just hoping for some legitimate respect.

We took a few days off in order to commemorate the death of the Shabdrung, the seventeenth-century founder of the state of Bhutan. During this time, without the agenda of climbing into and out of vans, I had time to breathe, to consider my own way of seeing things in relation to all I had seen and heard, how much of it had to flow past me as I translated it all into something comprehensible to other Westerners. I thought about how Western minds are fragmented. We understand ourselves according to basic laws of physics and consider things that are separated from each other in space or in time to be separate things, which seems reasonable and necessary to go about our daily lives. But in Bhutan that's not a necessity. There's a fluidity to life in Bhutan. In Bhutan, people flow back and forth easily between what we call myth and what we call reality in explaining everyday life and explaining their history: a combination of recorded historical events, legends, and religious texts and oral stories.

These events, whether real or not from a Western perspective, impact how Bhutanese to this day understand their history, and thus who they are as a people in relationship to themselves and to the rest of the world.

One might wonder why the Bhutanese think this way, but maybe the question is why do we think the way we do? Why do we need to winnow out the empirical evidence to comprehend something as true? Now, that's not to say that empirical experience should be overlooked. My feet are genuinely on the table as I write this on my laptop, a metal machine made three years ago by a company named Apple. But the stories that I know hardly anything about— the way that the deities settled a valley, their interactions with the Buddhist pioneers in the area, and the relationships both have had with the people who have lived there, over millennia—are equally valid interpretations of events. They have as much, if not more, of an impact on people's lives and directs how they lead them than anything that I might consider more real. I am a tangential person to the lives of people here, because I stand outside the constant and daily interactions that they have with each other, their karmic cycle of rebirth, and the overarching relationships they have with their Buddhist priorities, in tandem with the guardian deities they consider in all their decisions in their lives.

There is a room in human minds that the Bhutanese still have access to. It's an interesting place that I've seen from the outer gates time and again in my travels, but which I am never able to fully enter. I remain unaware of the forces at work around me and how they affect me, and how I affect them. Perhaps, because of my limited way of seeing the world, I'm the one that's not entirely real.

Chencho helped me delve into this intersectional place that I tried to understand, where the messengers of the deities and the messengers of the hell realms of Buddhism reside. The common background stories tell the tale of clerical Buddhism overcoming and converting local deities but continuing to tolerate them, since they remain useful for Himalayan society.

In our conversations, I learned that the so-called minor deities are really much more central to religious life in Bhutan than I thought. To be clear, there is no question that the Bhutanese are devout Buddhists; they undoubtedly are. Bhutanese Buddhism on the one hand is like a set of guidelines for life and on the other hand is integrated into a system of worship of Buddhist figures and deities that reflect the principles of those guidelines: how to properly interact with the environment and with each other with compassion. It is a fully lived religious culture. I find myself reflecting on the difference between their culture and my own, and I realize that though I wish I could fully be part of something so vital, organic, and well lived, I never will

Françoise, Chencho, and I honored the Shabdrung day of commemoration by visiting the Tashicho Dzong in Thimphu. Dzongs combine a central monastery with political offices. They are grand and beautiful stone buildings imbued with history, and gorgeous iconography covers the walls and hallways that serve as the entrances. Watching people coming to the temple on this holy day was an immersive experience into this organic world. The willow trees were bending with the weight of their new green leaves and California poppies were blooming in the wide beds along the walkway to the monastery.

Extended families dressed in their finest clothes, from the smallest children to the oldest grandmothers, made their way through the long, ornately painted hallways to the large open-air courtyard, stopping to take group photos with the tall whitewashed monastery walls as a backdrop. The monks went about their daily business of maintaining the temple and its grounds, their maroon robes swirling around their ankles. Above the courtyard walls was the piercingly blue springtime sky. The beautiful afternoon needed no more embellishment to proclaim itself as sacred in its quietness and isolation from the day-to-day.

After the three of us parted ways I made my way back to my hotel room and changed into jeans and a sweater before heading out for lunch and, as it turns out, most of the rest of Thimphu was also going out for lunch. It was a holiday, so huge family groups were amassing in all the local places. My solitary lunch next to a large table in a second-floor restaurant was happily invaded by a family of ten, and soon I was drowned in their family chatter, with occasional warm inquiries directed to me in English, embracing my presence without any extra fuss.

12

THE DIVINE MESSENGER OF THIMPHU

The following year, I returned to Bhutan. Françoise found out that the Paro khandrom had now also moved to Thimphu. A German tour guide was bringing groups of interested foreigners to her. Françoise tracked down her address, and we drove there to meet her. Her apartment was located in a maze of streets lined by new concrete buildings that have sprung up on the southern outskirts of Thimphu, on a hill overlooking the town.

When we arrived, a young woman was hanging clothes on a line. When they saw us, several young kids who were playing in front of her door quickly dispersed. The young woman asked us to wait there, in the little cement walled portico until the khandrom was ready for us, so we chatted with her in English while we waited. She told us she was from southern Bhutan and that when she and the khandrom met, the khandrom immediately recognized her as her sister. The girl said she was so honored that she decided to spend her time working for the khandrom.

The girl was unusually dressed for a religious engagement, at least by Bhutan standards: instead of a kira she wore jeans and a T-shirt, lipstick, and eye shadow. Eventually she showed us into a parlor with a couch, table, and chair, where the khandrom eventually joined us. She told us that Thimphu was working out better for her financially. It's a big city, so she was getting more visitors, she said, including tour groups. She told us that once, a foreigner asked her to heal a sick friend back in Germany via Skype, and she was able to do it. She seemed more assured about her role as a healer now. Although she knew we were coming, she didn't change into her religious robes. There was no incense.

Departing

I have gotten on a plane in Bhutan to fly home possibly seven times over the past decade. Each visit there is a snapshot—a picture of how things are the last time I was there—and I carry that feeling and those internal images with me like a set of still photographs, where nothing changes once the picture has been taken.

But Bhutan is nothing if not changing. And every time I return, the changes are so immense and extraordinary that I find it hard to relocate the place I carried around inside my head since the last time I was there.

In Thimphu, hotels are being built and old reliable meeting places have been abandoned for new meeting points. Outsiders flow into the city like a river, and each new person that arrives creates a change that can often only be recognized long after their departure.

The early morning light is sifting through my guesthouse windows as I pack my bag to prepare to leave. I hear the ravens in the trees and in the yard, and the cars beginning to rumble through town. In the house next door a ceremony is starting up; perhaps a ritual for someone in the family who died. I can smell the incense and hear the drone of the sacred horns and the sound of the monks chanting scripture. After our immersion into the world of these divine messengers, I begin to see some patterns and begin to make sense of it all.

There has always been a renegade aspect to the life of divine messengers. Of the messengers we know about, none of them chose their path: it found them. Once they became known as a divine messenger, a female shaman, there was no going back. They became a backbone of authority that existed separately from the accepted authority of the Buddhist monastery. As an authority that was not commonly acknowledged by the monastery, they charted their own path. The authority they gained in their community was derived from the effectiveness of their advice and rituals, not from an elevated status. As women who could not go to school, this was a clear pathway forward for legitimacy.

No matter how careful one is, coming to a place as an outsider can leave big holes in understanding the fullness of what it is to be human and what it is to be a messenger of the divine. My words can do little to change that, except to say I do agree with Samten Karmay when he talks about a place where human minds can go, where the interior landscape looks nothing like what we can see with our eyes. There are people, including deloms and their successors, who inhabit this interior landscape almost full-time. Their decisions start there: from a place that I have never been allowed access to—a place of complete interconnection between the deities and humans, between the visible and invisible, among the energies so abundant in the world in its unmeasured state.

Because of their position within this landscape, perhaps the women we met have been able to understand that commonality of life more easily than other people. They are professional outsiders to normal society, which could make it easier to offer empathy and an outsider's eye to the problems of the people who seek their advice. And perhaps women might have more of a tendency to go into this realm if they are denied access to the clear path of authority in the realm of the day-to-day. This place, this world, appears to offer a solution of identity for women who appear as "misfits," for women who do not fit in the social norms, who would rather follow a spiritual path, and who want to play a beneficial role for people in this lifetime. However we shouldn't forget that they don't engage in this path freely. They are called to this role by forces that do not leave them any choice. Legitimate authority in Vajrayana Buddhism largely comes from being a reincarnation of a venerated teacher. Perhaps the divine messengers are indeed turning into a venerable, accepted form of lineage holders in their own right.

While the nyenjoms continue the work of placating the local deities with shamanic practices, the deloms today seem inclined to cast aside the shamanic practice of dying and returning from the dead. Transforming from delom into rizam, their roles have expanded. They no longer simply bring advice back from the hells, guide the living in how to live respectfully in their human form, or guide human actions on behalf of the dead.

The modern rizam is now consulted almost exclusively about advice for this lifetime. She has designated herself as a rizam or khandrom without input of the Buddhist monastic authority, or else the people who consult with her have conjectured those terms themselves. Her legitimacy rests on the usefulness of her advice, not on outside recognition.

The rizam has internalized Buddhist precepts herself, and now she divines for others accordingly. Buddhism and the need for divine advice are deeply interwined in the life of the Bhutanese.

I can feel my stomach unsettled, gnawing in preparation for the sadness I know I am about to feel arriving at the airport in Paro. This departure is no different. The stories of the divine messengers can so easily vanish as soon as I step on the plane. But instead of allowing them to vanish, perhaps it's up to me now to see the world differently. It's on me to understand that the liminal place where the shaman lives between worlds has many access points. Perhaps it's up to me to embrace even the glimpses I might catch of the wholly interconnected world where we all truly live, however we inhabit it, and to allow that to be what's real.

As much as this place changes, there is always an ineffable something here. It feels like a dispute long since settled, a plan long since laid. There is a comfort and predictability in Bhutan's extreme isolation in the midst of the highest mountains in the world. The world comes to Bhutan at Bhutan's convenience. I hope that it is always this way.

PART THREE

A Delom Biography
in Translation

The Life Story of Sangay Choezom

Delom Sangay Choezom was already mentioned in this book. She was a delom from eastern Bhutan who lived probably at the beginning of the eighteenth century. Françoise translated her biography into French and published it in 1989 as part of her PhD dissertation, and Richard Whitecross kindly translated it into English. We present here the most relevant parts of this biography and the voice of this historical delom to provide a better frame for the religious context of the women we interviewed.

OM MANI PADME HUM HRIH

The absolute nature, pure from the beginning,
Is totally free from elaboration and concepts.
I pay homage to the body of the essence, Amitabha,
The unalterable heart, the nature equal to the Victorious.

From absolute space, uncreated and totally pure,
Arises an expression of the creativity of the omnipresent wisdom.
I pay homage to the enjoyment body, Avalokiteshvara,
The spontaneous clarity and omnipresent mandalas of the
    Victorious.

In the immensity of the pure unity
Shines the light of the sun of great compassion.
I pay homage to the body of transformation, the Lord of the Dead,
Yama Dharmaraja,
Who illuminates the darkness of the ignorance of sentient
    beings.

He sees all beings of the six destinies with his compassionate eyes
And holds in his heart the union of wisdom and emptiness,
Which disperses the suffering of all sentient beings.
I pay homage to Avalokitshvara Mahakaruna.

In order to accomplish the temporary happiness and ultimate
    bliss of sentient beings,
The Wisdom dakini manifests as the unity of the knowledge and
    tenderness of all Buddhas.
I pay her homage,
For she accomplishes the Four Activities without which nothing
    stops.

Embrace the fire of the end of time
On the order of the Buddha and the assembly of dharma
    protectors and guardians
who uphold the teachings.
I pay homage to them and to their retinues who liberate the ten
    objects to be liberated.

OM MANI PADME HUM HRIH

Now, the incarnation of Avalokiteshvara, the delom Sangay Choezom, will recount the merits of delivery from the six realms in
which beings follow the law of retribution for actions [cause and
effect, karma]. Having descended to the Eighteen Hells, she will
in particular recount the fashion by which beings in the six realms
suffer as retribution for their actions, and how among the living
beings on earth, Yama Dharmaraja, the Lord of the Dead, and the
dead themselves exhort them:

· The lazy to practice religion (dharma),
· The avaricious to make gifts and donations,
· The angry, the proud, and the envious to cultivate a spirit
    of compassion,

- The sinners to confess their faults, after which the terror will arise in them,
- The people to profoundly venerate their parents, who are their benefactors; their friends; the Dorje lopon [Vajra lama] and the lamas; and to show compassion without having for a moment any idea or intention to cause harm to any being in the six realms.

The delom will also in particular recount the means by which the Lord of the Dead counts the virtuous and non-virtuous deeds, the sufferings of the Eighteen Hells, and the message that the Lord of the Dead gave to her. All of this will be explained for the benefit of all.

For those who hear this biography, it is important to respect these three promises: not to tell the biography, even if it is known already; to listen without distraction; and finally not to chatter inconsiderately. It is vital to listen and to follow these three pieces of advice.

Here then is the story of her life.

In Bhutan, in the province of Trashigang, in a place called Phagri Sangdung, lived a man called Sonam Dondup and his wife, Tsewang Gyalmo, who possessed all of the signs of being a Wisdom dakini. They had a daughter, Sangay Choezom, who was the incarnation of Avalokitshvara. When she was twelve years old, on the twenty-third day of the sixth month of the Year of the Dog, a man appeared and said, "This girl possesses the signs of being a Wisdom dakini. In a previous life, she was the delom Karma Wangzin."

OM MANI PADME HUM HRIH.

Now, here is the dream which I, the delom, had: In the Year of the Pig, on the twenty-fifth day of the sixth month, a white man appeared to me and pronounced these words: "O, daughter, if you act in a pure manner, this is a prophecy that concerns you. You will visit the Eighteen Hells. If you do not act in a pure manner, you will only live for seven days." I was happy because it was not a man; it was Avalokitshvara in person who had come to meet me.

Another night, in a dream, I thought I was in the house of my father and there appeared before me five frightening faces: white, yellow, red, green, and blue (the Five Victorious Buddhas). I saw these terrifying beings around me and at that moment I felt a great fear. I thought: "If I am dead, I am with my carnal body (corpse). If I am not dead, none of my parents, siblings, or relatives are here." And suddenly I realized that my maternal uncle and people I had known before who were all now dead were also present. I realized at that moment that I was dead, and tears flowed down my cheeks. A white man with a very white face appeared and said to me, "You are not dead, don't cry." He took me by my right hand and ordered me to follow him, and we left by the door. He guided me on an inde-scribable path, and we arrived at the foot of a high, black mountain. As we rested, I said to him "Where should I go since I no longer have a friend?"

On the black mountain stood a black tree on which I saw all sorts of donors making offerings. This vision was pleasant, and I asked my guide about the mountain. The white man replied, "If you remember this mountain, it is Mount Potala. If you do not remember this mountain, it is a black mountain." Then, leading me, he began to climb. We arrived at a temple located at the upper part of the mountain. A red man appeared and said to me, "Daugh-ter, where are you going?" I replied, "I came to visit the temple." He said, "Since the duration of your life is not yet exhausted, return."

I returned to my home in a day, and I heard my parents saying that I was dead and that they were struck with immense sadness. I asked them, "What those people, real and unreal, said in my dream is correct. I must therefore die now. Is it because of the prophecy from my previous life or is my current life the cause?" My parents replied, "Daughter, your current life is not the cause. There is a prophecy from your previous life."

On the thirtieth day of the sixth month of the Year of the Dog, early in the morning, the symptoms of my death began to appear, and I felt as if the sun was going down, that darkness was approaching and that my body was no longer my own. A great sadness gripped me, and I began to cry. At that moment, my mother rose and said, "Daughter, why are you crying?" I said to her, "Today, I do not want to eat and I do not want to drink. The time has come for me to be separated from you, my parents, from my family, and I shall be alone." My parents then said, "Some time ago, somebody said that you are the reincarnation of the delom Karma Wangzin. If you want to return, we will look after your body. If you do not, we will not look after it."

They wrapped my body in a clean white cloth and offered flowers, incense, and butter lamps. Seven people kept watch over me day and night, carefully reciting the Mani mantra [OM MANI PADME HUM HRIH, which liberates from the different reincarnations]. My parents gave them this order: "If she does not return in seven days after her departure to the other side, she will return in fifteen days. If she does not return after fifteen days, destroy her corpse."

OM MANI PADME HUM HRIH.

THE CHAPTER ON THE HOT HELLS

When my body and my main consciousness became separated, it was as if thunder rumbled in the sky, rocks collapsed, and I entered into darkness. I felt the pain of thinking that I was dead and held the thought that I was not dead. I did not enter the darkness, and the moment arrived when my body separated from my spirit. In an instant, my main consciousness escaped through the crown of my head and I failed to recognize my body; I saw instead the body of a pig the size of a mountain. Tears flowed from my eyes. I arrived in front of my *yidam* (tutelary deity), and he said to me, "Do you not know that you are dead? Don't be attached to your illusion body, but rather raise your spirit toward the essence of phenomenon. Come where I lead you." He took my hand and guided me. We traveled everywhere in the sky, on the earth, and in space so that I did not know where we went. My yidam said to me, "Recite the

Mani mantra seven times." I recited the Mani mantra seven times, and the yidam guided me to a high black mountain obscured by black clouds. Innumerable cries of wrathful and peaceful deities rang out, "Kill, kill, execute, execute!" as well as sounds such as *"Hum, hum, phat, phat."* I lost consciousness from fear as I was very afraid. My yidam then took me by the hand and said to me, *"OM MANI PADME HUM HRIH.* If you do not remember, you will see a black mountain; if you do remember, you will see the Paradise of Buddha Vairocana. Further, if you go on, you will reach the foot of a white mountain, then a yellow mountain, then a red mountain, and finally a green mountain. If you remember these mountains, each is a paradise of the Five Victorious Buddhas; if you do not, they are the first *bardo* (state of existence between death and rebirth)."

On these mountains, I saw the terrible sufferings endured by the dead, who were being whipped in a black cloud by torrential rain and hail. This sight made me very unhappy, and I asked the yidam why the dead were enduring such suffering. My yidam replied to me, "When they were alive in the world, they cried and lamented when being blessed by meditators. This is the retribution for their actions. They will not be liberated from this black obscurity."

As we descended, we arrived at a black path, and there I saw an unimagined number of all sorts of dead from our world. I saw a host of vermin made up of living beings and lamas, mostly spiritual advisors. I asked my yidam where we were, and he replied that this path was where all beings of the six destinations come when they die.

On the path, I saw an old man wearing a white robe, howling as he progressed. He carried on his back a portion of meat the size of a mountain. I posed a question to my yidam, and he replied, "This is the punishment for acts of violence and theft that he committed when he was alive in the human realm. When he came to this realm, he arrived from that direction in the presence of the Lord of the Dead, who distinguished between his good deeds and his sins. He is going to the Hell of the Great Cauldron. He is from your country. His name is Apa Dargye." I asked what sort of virtuous actions I could do to liberate him. My yidam replied, "Perform propitiatory rituals to the divinities and purify the sins, recite a million times the Mani mantra and erect prayer flags. He will then be liberated from these sufferings."

We then descended to a green land, and I saw a large prayer flag. A stupa of five colors rested between two white stupas and two black stupas. At the foot of each stupa stood a white tree, a black tree, and a raised prayer flag. I asked about the stupas and the local town. My yidam replied, "The name of this place is the Great Town of the Country of the Dead. If you recognise the five stupas, these are the five paradises of the Five Victorious Buddhas." At the foot of the stupas on the black iron soil—and in a black cloud of iron—a man wept. I asked my yidam about this man, and he replied, "This is the punishment for having killed insects and birds when he was alive. From now on, he will live in an iron house.

I also saw a man dressed in red who was carrying on his back a sacred book. I asked my yidam where the man was going, and he told me, "That man recited the words of the Buddha when he was on the earth. Due to his virtues, he is on the path of liberation which will lead him to paradise after meeting with the Lord of the Dead."

I also saw more people weeping with their faces turned toward the sun. Some wept while standing, others sitting; yet others seemed to be rejoicing. My spirit was deeply perturbed, and I asked who these people were. My yidam replied, "Those who are weeping a great deal recall their punishment for killing animals and for having pride, envy, desire, and avarice. Those who are happy practiced meditation and read dharma books. Through these actions, they wait for the Land of the Buddha."

Then we descended following a red path. We reached a land where all the mountains and hills, all the valleys high and low were white and pure. My divine yidam was white also and I, too, became white. There, all the deceased, with their bodies from the human realm, were also white. The rays of light were equally white and in this blazing light appeared the white face of a terrifying divinity. Dressed in green, the divinity held in its hand a black knot. As there were innumerable divinities in the sky whose cries resounded like thunder, I asked my yidam where we both had arrived. My yidam replied, "The deceased will travel here in one day and will arrive at this white place. If the deceased recognise it, it is the Paradise of Buddha Vajrasattva."

When we continued further, we met a terrifying yellow divinity, then a red one, then a green one; we met diverse terrifying divinities. I lost consciousness and collapsed. My yidam appeared before me with a white face, white clothes, and a rosary in his hand and said to me, "*OM MANI PADME HUM HRIH*. Ah, my daughter, stand up. The fears that exist within you are now manifested in this assembly of peaceful and terrifying deities. Have no fear and get up. What you see is what appears to all who have died during the five days following their death."

I continued to descend and arrived at a black bridge. A large rocky mountain overhung the bridge. Below was an immense ocean of fire. The bridge was so large that its length could not be measured even on horseback in eighteen days. On the opposite side of the bridge I met an acolyte (religious assistant) of the Lord of the Dead with the head of an ox. His face was very red, and he had three eyes. His hair was blue-gray, and he wore a tiger skin. He carried a lance in his hand with which he struck the bound dead. Ox-head said to them, "The pork you ate was delicious, wasn't it?" I asked what actions they were being punished for, and my yidam replied, "It is their punishment for taking lives in order to eat meat when they were alive in the lands of countless humans." At this place I met lots of different animals: tigers, leopards, bears, monkeys, birds, boars, and so forth. These animals asked me, "Daughter, do you come from earth? Men took our lives; is there a chance that they will come here now? They should pay for our lives." Therefore, I, the daughter, said to them, "Among those who die when the course of their lives has ended, some will probably come here. They must pay for the lives of the different animals that they killed." The animals welcomed me, and I spent some time amongst them.

I then saw a woman dressed in blue who was crushed beneath a black mountain and many others enveloped by a black cloud. After watching these beings endure their suffering, a great compassion arose in me, and I questioned my yidam. He replied, "When they were alive, they profited from making beer. These sufferings are their punishment. They will not be free from their sufferings until a *kalpa* (eon) has passed."

We continued to descend, and I saw a white rock and a yellow rock, and I saw that we crossed two rivers, one red and one green. I asked my yidam about them. He replied, "*OM MANI PADME HUM HRIH*. Listen, my daughter. These white and yellow rocks that you see are the palaces of the virtuous and the sinners. The two rivers, red and green, are the streams of hell."

We then came across three different colored paths. The highest path was white, and I saw an acolyte with the head of a lion. The middle path was yellow, and I saw an acolyte with the head of a bull. The lower path was black, and I saw an acolyte with the head of a monkey. I asked my yidam about the three paths and which one we would take. He replied, "The white path leads to paradise." From the white path appeared an unbearable five-colored light. Then, from looking at the black path, I saw different towns. From the yellow path came a ray of six different colors. A profound sadness arose within me and tears fell from my eyes. My yidam said, "*OM MANI PADME HUM HRIH*. Alas, listen my daughter, the great sinners and the ignorant must realize the true nature of phenomena. This ray of white is that of the Buddha Vajrasattva; the yellow, Buddha Ratnasambhava; the red, Buddha Amitabha; the green, Buddha Amogasiddhi; and the blue, Buddha Vairocana. The ray of white that appears is the ray of the Buddha of the destiny of gods; the red ray, that of the destiny of demigods; the blue ray, that of the destiny of human beings; the green ray, that of animals; the yellow ray, that of the hungry ghosts; and the ray of smoke, that of the hell-realm. These six rays are the paths that you will follow, my daughter. The different towns that you see are called the Great Plains of the Land of the Dead, or the Eighteen Hells, or Great Towns of the Bardo. These are the towns of the acolytes of the Lord of the Dead.

We then went toward the west, leaving the yellow path, and arrived at the palace of the Lord of the Dead. The palace was built on black earth and surrounded by a black wall. Above it was a mountain of red flames, and it was covered by a tent of black smoke. On the four sides of the palace were the gatekeepers: in the east, the tiger-headed guardian; in the south, the pig-headed guardian; in the west, the lion-headed guardian; and in the north, the wolf-headed guardian. On either side of each of the gates, I saw on the right a guardian with the head of a bear shouting terrifying cries and on the left a guardian with the head of a dog shouting terrifying cries. An immense feeling of suffering arose within me and I fainted. My yidam said to me, "The frightening cries of the gatekeepers are the cries of mistaken illusion. Have faith and venerate the gatekeepers, they are the gatekeepers of the Lord of the Dead." Then my yidam and I entered the palace together. In the middle of a blue floor on a raised throne, the Lord of the Dead, with a red body and three eyes, looked at the sky. His long hair was dressed upon his head in five different colors, and he wore a necklace of dried skulls and a tall, flat hat. On his upper body he wore a brocade robe and on his lower body the skin of a tiger. In his right hand he held the Mirror of Deeds and in his left, he held a sword, water, and fire. His body was as large as a fiery red mountain and as high as eighteen mountains piled on top of each other. His voice resounded like a thousand thunder dragons.

To his right, I saw a little black demon with a black body and long red hair wearing a tiger skin. In his hands he held small black pebbles. An innumerable entourage circled around him. His body resembled Mount Sumeru.

To his left, I saw a white god with a white body. He wore on his head a "hat of life" and was dressed in clothes of white and green.

In his right hand, he held white pebbles and in his left a blue rosary; he recited the six-syllable mantra.

Before the Lord of the Dead I saw an acolyte with the head of a bull, a red body dressed in the skin of a tiger, and a black spear in his hand. I saw an acolyte with the head of a lion, a white body, turquoise-blue hair, and dressed in a tiger skin; he read a single red letter with a blue body, holding a sword.

There was an acolyte with the head of a tiger, with a black body, holding in his hands an axe.

There was an acolyte with the head of a dog, with a dark red body, holding in his hands a small bell.

There was an acolyte with the head of a bird, with a blue body, holding in his hands a war axe.

There was an acolyte with the head of a serpent, with a green body, holding in his hands a vase of lustrous water.

There was an acolyte with the head of a rat, with a dark red body, holding in his hands iron chains.

There was an acolyte with the head of a hare, with a yellow body, holding in his hands a hook.

There was an acolyte with the head of a monkey, with a dark red almost black body, holding in his hands a small set of scales.

There was an acolyte with the head of a sheep, with a green body, holding in his hands a mountain made of iron.

There was an acolyte with the head of a garuda, with a dark red body, holding in his hands a noose.

The size of the bodies of these innumerable acolytes almost equaled a mountain.

Among those who uttered such cries as "*Hum, hum, phat, phat,* execute, execute, kill, kill*," I saw those occupied with casting horoscopes, others holding a water clock, and others holding official lists, while others made the selection between virtuous and non-virtuous actions. I saw that as retribution for their actions, the dead were cut into pieces; sharp instruments filled the sky and fell upon the bodies.

The acolytes said to the Lord of the Dead, "Some have not seen the frightening apparitions of the bardo and have committed the sin of killing when they were in the land of the people. They killed many living beings. Their spirits are sullied by ignorance, anger, desire, indecent words, cupidity, pride, avarice, and maliciousness, all of which they violently repent when they arrive here. They faint and fall facedown on the ground. When they collapse, their mouths are twisted as they groan, 'Alas, alas!' This fear is not enough, and they must go to the different hells."

I then saw tears flow from their eyes. The acolytes said, "Some have practiced the dharma, read religious texts, followed the narrow path, made offerings to the Three Jewels, and given to beggars."

The Lord of the Dead said, "You virtuous ones and you sinners, look into my mirror of deeds." He called three times to an acolyte with the head of a bull and said, "Once the life of the sinners is exhausted, they arrive in my presence. I look in my mirror of deeds and I see that they have not engaged in even one virtuous or moral act. On the contrary, they have committed many sins. You, tie a noose around their necks and now lead them to the hells."

As I saw the dead were very afraid, I fainted. When I recovered a little of my spirit and understood what I had seen and suffered, tears ran from my eyes. Then my yidam said to me, "*OM MANI PADME HUM HRIH.* Alas, my daughter, listen to me. The palace that terrifies the dead is the palace of the Lord of the Dead. The different acolytes that you see are his entourage. All those people who you see crying are receiving retribution for having killed living beings when they were alive. As for those people who have deep beliefs, they are receiving the benefit of having engaged in good actions."

At that moment, the yidam transformed himself into a person with a face white like a conch, wearing a divine robe and a black and green "hat of life." At the same time, I noticed that my body was not the same as it had been before. I understood that I had acquired a bardo body, which is not like a body of flesh and blood. I distinctly recalled my previous lives, and I recognized the god as my own yidam. I then thought that when I was on earth in this life, I had not performed any virtuous actions, and I did not know what virtuous or non-virtuous actions I had committed in my previous lives. I now felt very afraid of the acolytes. Abundant tears flowed from my eyes. The Lord of the Dead said to me, "*OM MANI PADME HUM HRIH.* You, daughter of the earth, during your eleven previous lives you have incarnated without mistake in your line and that of your parents, and you have arrived here today. Observe well for seven days the sufferings of the Eighteen Hells below, the Paradise of Liberation above, and between the two the distinction of virtuous deeds and sins carried out by the acolytes and the sufferings that the dead endure. Be the messenger between the living and the dead for those on earth."

I was then named Delom Sangay Choezom, the revenant from beyond. The Lord of the Dead gave me numerous messages and said to me, "My daughter, tour the Eighteen Hells for seven days and then return to the land of men."

I saw a man dressed in yellow. The acolyte with the head of a bull tied a noose around his neck and tied his hands behind his back; the many acolytes all cried, "*Hum, hum, phat, phat;* execute, execute, kill, kill!" and they struck him with hammers. I asked what he had done to receive such a terrible retribution, and my yidam said, "He has committed sins," and called out to the acolytes, "Hey, acolytes, listen! Loosen the ties on that man and release him. You, do you have a message to give to the land of men?" The acolytes loosened the chains slightly and the man said, "You, my daughter of good karma, if you return to the land of men, please give them this message. I am from western Bhutan, from Punakha, and my name is Depa (chief) Drukgyal. When I was alive, I accumulated many sins. Now I am in the hells, subject to sufferings beyond imagination. My younger brother is called Dorje Namgyal. To help me, tell him that he must erect one hundred statues of the Buddha Aksobhya—support of the Body of the Buddha; he should commission a written copy of the Kanjur—support of the Word of the Buddha; he must erect one hundred Enlightenment stupas—support of the Wisdom-Mind of the Buddha; and he should erect one hundred prayer flags with the six-syllable mantra printed on them. He should make many offerings for the ceremonies of the transfer of merit and long life. Also, he should venerate yogis, both men and women, and give them lots of alms. He should copy for me the text of the *Vajracchedika* and the text of the *Contrition of Sins*. He should make offerings to the Three Jewels with the one hand and to the poor with the other. If he does these virtuous actions, I will be delivered from suffering. If he does not, I will have to continue suffering. The present lord in the land of men should not mistreat others, nor commit the sins that I have. Give this message such as it is to the living." I then saw the acolytes retie his chains as before and lead him to the hells.

The yidam and I continued toward the bottom of the red road. As we arrived at a black path, I saw an acolyte with the head of a monkey holding a black noose; he bound the dead before taking them away. I asked the yidam where these people were going, and he replied that they were going to the bardo, the Land of the Dead.

As we descended, we then came to a red place. I saw the acolytes seize each person by the hands and feet and take them into a great cloud of black iron. They were crying and lamenting but to no avail. I saw them bound by the hands and feet with iron chains. I saw those sitting beneath prayers flags weeping. I saw those rejoicing and those carrying posts for prayer flags. As I watched these people enduring all sorts of suffering, I asked my yidam what sins they had committed to suffer so. He replied, "*OM MANI PADME HUM HRIH*. Alas, listen well, my daughter. The name of this town is Bardo, Land of the Dead. The people in the iron cloud wounded others with their hard words. Those bound with iron chains killed animals that they had first trussed up and then tied their limbs. Those weeping beneath the prayer flags are weeping because the living have not performed any virtuous actions to help them. Those who are happy and rejoicing are benefiting from having raised prayer flags. The others that you see carrying the standards are doing so because they did not carry out a consecration ceremony. Those suffering here will not be liberated until a kalpa has passed.

I saw an old woman dressed in red who was in the black iron

cloud, crying, "Waa, waa." I asked what sins this woman had committed to suffer this retribution. My yidam said to me, "This is the punishment for uttering calumnies and ill words when she was alive, and it is also the punishment for having kept for herself what she should have offered in alms."

As we descended, we arrived at a black path. I saw an immense black place inhabited by beings with three heads; they lit a hearth on which they placed a large red cauldron almost as large as Mount Sumeru. To the right of the cauldron, I saw a being with the head of a pig, a blue body, and a bellows that he used to stoke the fire. To the left of the cauldron I saw a being with the head of a garuda and a white body holding a bellows, and I saw the great brazier beneath the cauldron in flames. Through the top of the cauldron I saw a bronze liquid with reddish waves passing across the surface. To the right of the cauldron I saw beings with the heads of elephants and red bodies who held chains in their hands; they strangled the dead and threw their bodies into the cauldron. To the left of these I saw beings with the heads of tigers and black bodies seize the dead by their hands and feet and throw them into the cauldron. The acolytes said to the dead, "It was good not to eat raw meat when you were in the land of many people. It was good not to drink warm blood. Now, is this retribution agreeable?" I saw their skin and bones cooked until they separated. Once they were cooked, I saw them leave the cauldron and then be thrown back in again. I saw that there were numberless acolytes around the cauldron and innumerable beings in the cauldron. I saw acolytes stuff the beings' own skin in their mouths. I saw those struck by black iron hammers. I saw those placed on a small scale by an acolyte with the head of a monkey. I saw those stamped on by a great horse and those crushed under a rock the size of a mountain. I saw sufferings beyond imagination. I was very weary; tears fell from my eyes in an uncontrollable way.

I asked my yidam, and he said to me, "*OM MANI PADME HUM HRIH*. Alas, listen well. The Great Cauldron that you see is for cooking the sinners. Beings caught by the creature with the head of a bull are placed in the cauldron as a punishment for killing pigs and birds. Beings caught by the creature with the head of a tiger are placed in the cauldron as a punishment for killing goats and sheep. Those who have raised animals as if they were their own children and then kill them suffer without measure. They will not be delivered from the cauldron until a kalpa has passed. Many cry from thinking about the sufferings they will experience when thrown into the cauldron. Those whose skin is put into their own mouths are being punished for eating the hearts of living beings. Those struck by the iron hammers are being punished for mistreating other people. Those placed on the scales by the being with a monkey's head are those who used false scales and weights. Those being trampled by the great horse rode horses, and those crushed by the slabs of stone are being punished for placing heavy weights on animals who could not plead for themselves.

I saw a great black cauldron, and also blue, dark red, and green cauldrons as large as mountains. In them, a bronze liquid with waves moved across the surface. Around each cauldron were acolytes—innumerable in number—who used their bellows. The acolytes seized the dead and placed them in the cauldrons. All around the edge innumerable beings endured their sufferings. I again asked for what previous faults were these sufferings being endured. The yidam replied, "*OM MANI PADME HUM HRIH*. Alas, alas, listen well. Those in the black cauldron killed other humans by using weapons such as arrows and spears. They will not be free for three hundred thousand years. Those in the blue cauldron lived in castles and are from the race of all-powerful lords. This is their punishment for abusing their power, pronouncing bad words, taking that which was not given, and stealing and striking people dead. They will not be released for one thousand years. Those in the green cauldron are being punished for having eaten various different animals which they raised and then killed. They will not be delivered for one hundred years.

I saw at this place a mountain of weapons, their tips pointing upward to the sky. An acolyte with the head of a bear, a black body, and a curved iron sword in his hand seized a woman dressed in red by the throat and put her on the mountain; when she landed on the summit of the mountain, the tips of the weapons pierced her through from below and then pierced her through from above. At this place I heard cries of "*Han, han!*" from beings without bodies, and I then asked what actions caused this retribution. My yidam replied to me, "*OM MANI PADME HUM HRIH*. Alas, my daughter, listen. This great mountain of weapons is the storage chest of Shalmali. This acolyte with the head of a bear is the gatekeeper of Shalmali. This nun dressed in maroon is called Lhawang Zompa and she is from the east of Bhutan. When on the earth, she asked for many teachings and transmissions from a kind lama. However, she acted against the teachings and broke her vows; she gave birth to a son. She did not show him to anybody, and she killed him herself. The nun is suffering this retribution for having killed her own child. She will not be free from this suffering before the end of a kalpa. The beings without bodies whose cries you hear, when they were on the earth, they favoured certain of their children to the detriment of their other children. They will not be released from Shalmali. When the nun arrived at the foot of Shalmali, the cries and the tears of her child reached her from the summit. When she heard his cries, the hour of their reunion did not sound. Each day her body is reconstituted twenty-one times, as she ascends and descends, and she experiences such sufferings without respite for her deliverance. This is the punishment of this mother for having killed her son.

There I also saw a black mountain of fire on top of which burned a large red rock, with a man lying down on his back, squashed by a cow the size of a mountain. This cow ate the heart of the man and drank his blood. I asked the yidam about this, and he replied, "The great red rock that you see is also called the land of great obscured and black hells. That man who is squashed under the cow has incurred this punishment because of his treatment of the cow. The man whose blood the cow drinks and heart the cow eats incurred this retribution for having maltreated the animal."

I saw an acolyte with the head of a deer and a green body tie up a man dressed in black by the neck with a black iron chain and crush him under a rock. I asked what action this man had done to incur this retribution. My yidam replied, "This man being crushed under a large boulder of iron incurred this punishment for having sold beer to members of the *sangha* (community of monks). Other men have their hearts pierced by a red iron needle, which that acolyte with the head of a pig and a blue body holds in his hand; they suffer this punishment for having been envious of the religious people and wishing them harm when they were in the land of human beings."

I saw an acolyte with the head of a dragon and a yellow body holding in his hand a black cord that bound, behind his back, the hands of a man who looked like an ordained monk. He was leading him, saying that he would throw the man into the great infernal cauldron. I asked why this man should incur such retribution. My yidam spoke to the acolytes, "You, acolytes, listen. This man is religious. What sort of actions did he commit when he was in the land of men, to incur this retribution? Does he have a message to send back to his land?"

The acolytes then said, "This man, while he has the appearance of a religious person, committed many sins. He ate a lot of food destined for the dead, and he also profited greatly from the wealth of a local lord. When he was small, he killed a bird without making penitence; however, he also conferred initiations to others. The punishment for these actions is to be placed in the Great Cauldron." And instead of beating him, they loosened his bindings a little so that he could give me his message. "Alas, alas, daughter of good karma, listen to me. As they say you will return to the land of men, this is what to say. I am from Trashigang, and my name is Tsering Karchung. My mother is called Tashi Choezom. For my salvation, she should copy one thousand times the *Vajracchedika* texts and the *Contrition of Sins*. She should offer many times one hundred butter lamps in the temples. She should erect a large prayer flag inscribed with the excellent six-syllable mantra. For the purification of my sins, she should perform the ritual of expiation of sins, the ritual of transfer of merit, and a prayer of blessing. So, you, my mother who loves your child, you will do these good deeds for my well-being and I will be reborn in the land of human beings. If you do not do these deeds, then I will not be free from this cauldron for one hundred years. Give this message on the earth." I saw the other acolytes bind him as before and take him away to the cauldron.

I saw there an acolyte with the head of a wolf and a black body who held in his hand an iron hook with which he led a woman dressed in red. An acolyte with the head of a bull took her away, hitting her with a black hammer. She wept and beat her chest with her fists, moaning "Alas, alas." I asked about which actions incurred this retribution. My yidam replied, "This being was the mother of a lord. Listen, acolytes! This being—loosen her binds a little. What sins has she committed? As there are those who want to undertake the necessary good actions to purify their sins, let her send a message back to the earth." The acolytes replied, "When this being was on the earth, it had the body of a woman but committed many sins such as killing, wasting the riches of the lord, and mistreating the servants. Her spirit was filled with pride, anger, and envy. We acolytes, we don't have much power. Generally, beings are sent down weighted by sin, and we place them in the cauldron. Furthermore, if that suffering is not enough, we take them to the Hell of Black Lines, and they will not be free before three hundred thousand years have passed."

This woman then said the words, "*OM MANI PADME HUM HRIH.* Alas! You, daughter of the earth, as they say you will return to the earth, take this message with you. My place of birth is the capital of the east of Bhutan. My name is Chokyi Lhamo. I have a great-nephew whom I raised named Palden Senge. To purify my sins, my whole family should erect a statue of Akshobhya as the Body support of the Buddha; they should have the Kanjur read as the Speech support of the Buddha; they should whitewash many stupas; and they should copy the *Vajracchedika* and *Contrition of Sins* texts. They should offer gifts to the lama for the ritual of the transfer of merit and provide services to the sangha. They should offer gifts to the *manipa* (itinerant lama who go from village to village with their portable altars) for the transfer of merit and anything necessary for the rituals. They should provide to a living yogi in retreat the objects necessary for reciting well the six-syllable mantra. They should make offerings to the lamas, yidams, and dakinis with faith and respect. They should be good and feel compassion toward all beggars who wander the country. My beautiful clothes and jewelry should be given to accomplish good actions. Tell the most powerful lord in the land not to beat people unjustly and tell all the lords to honestly keep order and apply the laws. I, the old woman with bad karma, I never accumulated good karma—people should not commit sins as I did! People should recite the Mani mantra, thinking that it is for the benefit of the future lives of all. If they are capable of reciting and doing good actions, they will be reborn as humans on the Continent of the West. If they have had a little happiness and pleasure on the earth, these people will not have an instant of happiness when they arrive in the hells. Deliver this message from the old woman that I am."

And straightaway I saw the acolytes with the head of a bull and the head of a wolf tie her and lead her away to the Great Cauldron. *OM MANI PADME HUM HRIH.*

When we went down, I saw on a red path an acolyte with the head of an owl and a blue body, who held in his right hand a garland of skulls and in his left hand a sword on the point of which was the corpse of a man. I saw in front of this acolyte a man dressed in blue with a white scarf covering his head, and this man was cut into small pieces from head to foot with a sword. A great sadness and immense pain filled me, and I asked what sins this man had committed. My yidam replied, "This is a man who committed sins." He called out, "You acolytes, listen! This is the moment for this man to explain his sins. This man whose body is cut into small pieces, does he now have a message to send to the people on earth?" The acolytes said to the god, "This man who is cut into small pieces incurred his punishment for having killed many different types of animals. He committed the sin of taking what was not given, he committed the sin of taking without the authorisation of the lord. As a result of these sins, we are going to take him to the Great Cauldron of Hell and he will not be delivered from suffering for one thousand years." The man then spoke, "Alas, alas, daughter of the earth, as you will return to the earth, take this message. My land is Kanglung in eastern Bhutan, my name is Koche Lungpo, and my wife is called Norla Deden. You, my wife and my children, to purify all of my sins, have the texts of Expiation and the *Confession of Sins* read one thousand times. Raise a large prayer flag printed with the six-syllable mantra and have the *Vajracchedika* read one thousand times. Make many offerings to the Three Jewels. If you do these good actions, I will obtain rebirth. If you do not, I will certainly go to the hells below, to the Hell of Black Lines."

I then saw the acolyte with the head of an owl bind and lead him to the Great Cauldron. *OM MANI PADME HUM HRIH*.

The edges of the Great Cauldrons were covered on all sides by swirling red storms. In the cauldrons, waves of black liquid bronze swept across the surface. (The tenth, fifteenth, and thirtieth day of each month were fast days in the lands of hell. On those days, the red storms and bubbling liquid bronze became calm. Even sinners with heavy karma in the Hell of Unceasing Tortures, all humans, and other living beings could be freed then.) At that moment I saw a man dressed in red and white, holding in his right hand a prayer wheel and in his left prayer beads; he circled the Great Cauldron three times. He then knocked over the green cauldron, walked up three steps of the golden staircase, and addressed the beings. "*OM MANI PADME HUM HRIH*. Hey! I have come to lead to paradise those dead who are from the land of men. In case the dead do not know me, let me present myself: I am Manipa Sherab Tenzin. Those who are connected to me by food and religious instruction, those who have made offerings of items for the ritual of transfer of merit and necessary ritual ornaments, those who have given me food and service, I am going to lead them to the Paradise of Potala, the Paradise of Avalokiteshvara. Those with a karmic connection to me, stand up! The sinners with heavy karma who have not accumulated virtue and are in the Great Infernal Cauldron below, let them stand up after abandoning their attachments—I will lead them to the western Paradise of Buddha Amitabha. Those who endure the sufferings of the Hell of Black Lines in the Iron Mountains down below, let them stand up after abandoning their pride—I will lead them to the Paradise of Kubera. Those who disobeyed their parents and monks and who are in the Towns of the Hells below, after abandoning their envious spirit—I will lead them to the Paradise of Buddha Aksobhya. Those who were greedy and are in the darkness of the hells below, those who endure the sufferings of the Hell of Lamentation and Tears, let them stand up after abandoning their greed—I will lead them to the Paradise of Guru Rinpoche. Those whose bodies are flayed in the Towns of Weapons below, let them stand up after abandoning their desire and hatred—I will lead them to the Paradise of Akanistha. Those who did not distribute their riches among men but stole from others, and endure the sufferings of the Trespasses and hunger and thirst in the Eighteen Hells below—they will be reborn in the presence of Avalokiteshvara.

I then saw those who endured the suffering of the Great Cauldron and the suffering of the Hell of Black Lines and the Wailing Hell—and the suffering of the Trespasses and those of the weapons and all the dead in the Eighteen Hells—all were liberated from unfortunate rebirths. The acolyte did not come to trap these people, and I saw that the dead who followed the manipa were liberated in the various paradises. I then saw naked crying people below the overturned cauldron. From the region of Lhasa in Tibet, there was a trader called Tsering Rabtan, a certain Ama Paldron, and the lord Kalzang Chogyal. Some came from Tsang: one was the chief of Tashilundrub disrict, the other was a nun named Ecung Buti. From the capital of Bhutan, there was the head of the district, Dorje, a woman called Sonam Palkyi, and a man called Karchung. From Tawang, there was Padma Tsering and Tsewang Paldron.

I saw them crying and lamenting to themselves, saying their

names and where they were from. The acolytes at that moment blew their bellows creating a great red storm. This storm swirled around, up high and down low, taking with it all the dead who remained. After watching these insupportable sufferings, I asked the yidam, "This man who overturned the cauldron, who led such uncountable numbers of people to paradise, and who has no fear of the dead or the acolytes, what good deeds did he do when he was on earth?"

My yidam replied to me, "*OM MANI PADME HUM HRIH*. Ha! You daughter of good karma, listen! When this man lived in the land of numerous people, he accomplished umpteen good actions. His name is Manipa Sherab Tenzin. He reached the top of the Golden Staircase of Three Steps and this signifies a man who has attained the third level of realization. He is capable of leading the dead to paradise. These actions are the result of his propagation of the excellent six-syllable mantra throughout the country. The dead who remain under the Great Cauldron have no connections, either by food or by religion, with this manipa. That is why they remain there, under the cauldron. He wrote the excellent six-syllable mantra on trees and on solid rocks, and he has received the benefits of these deeds. He built many *tashigomang* (portable chapels in the form of stupas with many doors of good fortune) to guide the living. He recited the six-syllable mantra three hundred thousand million times. The acolytes do not frighten him. He gains the benefit of having abandoned sin. That he exhorted all people, saying "Get up!" with a pleasant voice, shows that he is a reincarnation of Avalokiteshvara Mahakaruna. They will be reborn in the Paradise of Potala.

End of the first chapter of the hells.

OM MANI PADME HUM HRIH

The Chapter on the Cold Hells

The yidam and Sangay Choezom arrived finally at the shores of an ocean of warm blood. People who committed various sins are there enduring the appropriate torments. The same process of questions and answers as before allows the reader to know what happened.

From there we headed west where we arrived at a green place. The yidam said, "Look down here," and as I looked down, I saw the ground was frozen and icy; this was due to innumerable long kalpas of snow falling. The ground, surrounded by an expanse of water, revealed an acolyte with the head of a boar and a blue body, wearing a tiger skin; he was digging in the earth with his tusks while he led the dead bound by the throat with a black rope held in his hand. He placed them on the Snowy Mountain of Kalpas. I saw innumerable acolytes tie the hands of the dead behind their backs and push them forward. They made others move forward while striking them on the head; they were made to advance with their feet bound; they were made to move forward with a sword of iron at their throats; they were made to advance with their bodies constrained. I saw people enduring limitless sufferings of the intense cold. Some were naked, without clothing, their limbs shaking as they wept, with their heads on the ground. Others had their hearts crack due to the intense cold. Others, frozen by the fierce cold, saw their limbs fall off. Such tortures were without limit. These people said to me, "When we were on earth, we never saw the terrors of the bardo, and we committed a great number of sins. Now we have arrived here, and the retribution for our actions is our due. Alas, alas!" they wailed.

Some of them, when in the land of humans, failed to make offerings to the Three Jewels or to give to the poor. Out of greed they accumulated provisions and clothing. But arriving here, in the land of the bardo, all of that is like nothing. They suffer in the ice and snowstorms. At that moment, I experienced the suffering of the intense cold, and I felt profoundly sad. I asked why these people had to endure such terrible suffering.

My yidam answered thus, "*OM MANI PADME HUM HRIH*. Alas! my daughter, listen well! The Snow Mountains of Kalpa that surround this place are also called the Land of the Great Cold Hells.

That river, surrounded by a great ocean, is called the River of the Great Cold Hells. The acolyte with the head of a boar is the guardian of the gate to the Cold Hells in the Land of Hells. The numberless acolytes are the followers of the boar-headed acolyte. Those led forward with a cord around their necks caused suffering and tears when in the land of men. Those who have their hands tied behind their backs are experiencing this for having stolen clothing from other people. Those being hit around their head are suffering because they mistreated other human beings. Those whose hands and feet are bound with an iron chain are suffering for having treated animals in the same way. Those enchained around their waists are experiencing this retribution for avarice and for not wearing their own clothes, even when cold. Those who creep forward, held by their bodies, are suffering this punishment for having thrown animals into water. Those suffering from intense cold are being punished for having stolen clothes from statues. Those entirely nude—who are weeping with their heads on the ground—are experiencing this punishment for having stolen from the poor. Those people whose hearts crack are experiencing this for having stolen from the religious people. Those whose limbs are cut into pieces are experiencing this retribution for having put people into prison. Those who are battered by the ice and snowstorms are experiencing this punishment for failing to give clothing; while on the earth they possessed lots of clothes and brocades, but at the moment of death their clothes were thrown away like rags. Only on arriving in the land of the bardo did they recall their clothes and brocades. You, my daughter, will not feel the suffering of cold due to your karma in this life. All the dead here will not be free before a kalpa has passed."

The yidam once again addressed the acolytes. "Listen to me, you acolytes! In this place encircled by great mountains of snow are those who endure numerous tortures of cold. During the time when they were in the land of human beings, what sins did they commit to earn these punishments? Is there no way to liberate them from these sufferings? There is somebody who will soon return to the land of humans, and if one of them would like to send a message, he can give it to her." The acolytes replied, "The people from the earth who arrive here are those who have been charged; they experience these punishments because of their own sins. We acolytes, we do not have the power to charge or free them."

A naked being stood up in the midst of the great storm of ice and snow, beating her chest with both hands, and said the following words: "Alas, my daughter of good karma, as he said that you will go to the land of human beings, carry my message to the world. I was born near Bumthang, my birth village is called Chendebji, and my name is Ama Zangmo. When I was in the land of humans, I venerated the holy lamas, but I also said evil things about the holy sangha. I venerated the manipa who toured the country, but I quarreled with the villagers. I tried to perform some good actions; I raised prayer flags and recited the texts of the *Vajracchedika* and the *Confession of Sins*. Though I did not give generously to beggars who came to my door, I did offer them a full measure of grain so that they would not leave empty-handed. I undertook these actions, but the time finally arrived for me to experience my own death. The kalpa that will see my deliverance to paradise has not arrived. The acolytes have led me to this place of suffering in the Snow Mountains of Kalpa. Tell my children, all of my family, and also my eldest son, named Gomchen, to read the *Prajnaparamita* in sixteen volumes and to read the texts of *Vajracchedika* and The One Hundred Thousand Names of the Buddhas. They should raise prayer flags with the six-syllable mantra to purify my sins. They should offer one hundred butter lamps and one hundred sorts of food at temples where there are statues—the Body support of the Buddhas—and books—the Speech support of the Buddhas. If they do these good deeds, I will obtain rebirth in the world of humans. I have now spent eleven years in these hell realms, but my sufferings are not enough. If they do not complete these good actions, I will go to the Hell of Unceasing Tortures and I will not be free from that hell for ninety years. Take this message to the human realms. Tell them not to commit sins as I have done." After saying these words, she was led away as before.

To the north side of this snowy mountain, I saw the Lake of Cinders. On the perimeter I saw an acolyte with the head of a rat and a black body holding in his hand a red sabre. He plunged it into the heart of a man whom he then threw into the Lake of Cinders, and I also saw the innumerable followers of this acolyte.

This lake contained lots of naked people. The waves on the lake made frightening noises. The sinners were cooked until their skin and their bones became separated. Some bled from their noses and the blood ran into their mouths; others were struck on their heads by iron hammers; a flowing liquid carried ashes into the mouths of others. I saw innumerable beings tortured like this. I asked my yidam, and he replied to me, "*OM MANI PADME HUM HRIH*. Alas, daughter of mankind, listen! This Great Lake of Cinders that you see, it is the retribution for those who killed fish when they were in the world. Those who bleed from their noses experience this for having poisoned fish in the rivers. Those who are struck on the head by the iron hammers are experiencing this punishment for having cut off the wings of waterfowl. Those into whose mouths the ash runs are experiencing this punishment for having made business selling the fish that they killed. This is the punishment for having killed fish. They will only be released from the innumerable torments of the great lake of ash after a kalpa has passed.

A being with black skin came out of the lake and said these words: "Alas, alas, daughter of good karma! Because you will go to the land of humans, take this message to the earth. My land is Udzarong Yingkhar in eastern Bhutan. My name is Samdrup Phuntsok. When I was on the earth, I killed lots of fish, which are inoffensive animals. I killed lots of birds, deer, and wild beasts. Toward other people I displayed pride, envy, and anger. Though I had received the explanation of sins and virtues, I did not listen and committed many sins. The retribution for having accumulated these sins is to be put into the Great Lake of Cinders. Those people who are on earth should not kill the fish in the rivers. They should not kill the wild animals, the birds, and the deer. They should not commit the sins that I have committed." After having spoken, he was led into the lake.

The cold hells are finished.

OM MANI PADME HUM HRIH.

The yidam and Sangay Choezom head toward a place with large burning fires into which sinners are thrown. Further ahead, on a black mountain, are those who disobeyed their religious instructions and broke their vows. At last, the yidam and Sangay Choezom arrive at a lake of black poison into which those who committed the sin of taking poison are thrown.

The yidam then said to me, "Look toward the south." As I looked below, I saw a dark red lake with swirling waves and all around it were mountains of burning red iron. I saw black clouds of iron that billowed, and in front of all of this stood an acolyte with the head of a sea monster and a red body, wearing a tiger skin. He bound the dead by their feet with a chain of red iron and then threw them into the lake. I also saw the vast retinue of this acolyte. I saw people simmering in a broth of their own skins and bones and others whose heads were split by a black axe. Others were swallowing their own blood, while others still were being crushed by a great rock. After seeing such horrible sufferings as these, I asked my yidam, and he replied to me. "Alas, my daughter, listen well! This great lake surrounded by fiery mountains is the place where sinners are cooked. The acolyte with the head of a sea monster is the master of this great dark red lake. Those who are thrown into the lake tied up with a chain of red iron, when they were on the earth they killed many of the larvae that produce red pigment. Those who are struck on the head with a black axe experience this retribution for having sold the red pigment. Those in whose throats blood is poured are experiencing this retribution for dying the color red. Those crushed under a great rock experience this retribution for have worn clothes that were colored red. The people who have committed all these actions by using red pigment, they will not be freed from the lake for three kalpas."

Then, from among them appeared three men whom I knew. The man who appeared first said, "Daughter of mankind, why are you here? Have you come here after dying, or have you come for another reason?" I replied, "The hour of my death has sounded, and I have arrived here. As I must recount these stories on earth, the Lord of the Dead has instructed that I must return to the land of human beings. If you have a message, entrust it to me." The man then said, "Alas, alas, daughter of good karma, listen a moment. When I was in the land of the human beings, I killed many animals such as birds and pigs. The retribution for these acts is to be sent to the Hell of the Great Cauldron. I stayed there for a year. The punishment for having worked with red pigment is to suffer in this lake. Take this message to my son and my daughter. So that my sins can be purified, they need to read the texts of *Vajracchedika* and the *Confession of Sins*. They should raise a large prayer flag with the six-syllable mantra, and they should offer one hundred butter lamps and recite the *Confession of Sins* one thousand times. If they do these good actions, I will be reborn in the land of human beings in the body of a woman."

The man who followed him said, "My name is Yongba. Take this message to my wife and my children. This is the retribution for eating honey, which I took from beehives when I was in the land of human beings, and the retribution for many other sins is now to suffer in the lake. They should read the *Prajnaparamita* in sixteen volumes for the purification of my sins. They should request the gomchen (lay practitioner) who lives at the bottom of the valley to make water offerings to the hungry and thirsty beings in the hells. If you do these rituals of atonement, I will be reborn in the body of a goose."

Finally, the last man said, "My name is Sithar Drukgey. Take this message to my parents and to my brothers and sisters. The retribution for having (mistreated) cows when I was small and for having killed many animals is to suffer in the lake. The means to deliver me is for them to have the Kanjur read and for them to have the *Prajnaparamita* copied in twenty-five thousand verses, as well as the *Narak dong sprugs* (Overturning the Deepest Hells). If they do these practices for the purifications of sins, I will obtain rebirth in the Continent of the East. They should give all that they have to the Three Jewels and to the lamas. They should also give to mendicants. After abandoning sin, they should dedicate themselves to reciting the *mani* formula. Take this message to the land of human beings."

After having spoken, the three men were led again to the lake. *OM MANI PADME HUM HRIH.*

Sangay Choezom saw a lake of black smoke where those who had committed different types of sins were thrown. There she saw that those who had been malicious and those who had been angry were thrown into the lake of red blood. Beneath a mountain she heard the groans of those who were being crushed for disobeying and mistreating their parents.

We then went toward the northwest and climbed to the top of an iron staircase with five steps. My yidam told me to look below, where I saw a red expanse. All over were mountains of red iron in flames. In front, an acolyte with the head of a snake and a yellow body led the dead, who were bound at their waists by a rope of snakes which he held in his hand; he threw them onto the fiery mountains. All around was a retinue of innumerable acolytes. Also, there was an uncountable number of naked people, young and old. Some had heads bigger than their bodies, a head as large as Mount Sumeru. Their chests were like enormous mountains, their limbs as thin as stems, and their necks no thicker than a blade of grass. Fires burned from their mouths and limbs. As I watched the innumerable sufferings of these thirsty, hungry beings, I asked the god why were they enduring these sufferings. The yidam replied, "*OM MANI PADME HUM HRIH.* Alas, daughter of mankind, listen well! This town surrounded by red fiery mountains is also called the Land of Great Lamentations of Beings On Fire, the Land of Thirst.

This acolyte with the head of a snake guards the entrance to the Land of the *Preta* (*Yidag*/Hungry Ghosts). The preta are those beings who endure the sufferings of hunger and thirst. When they were on earth, a large quantity of goods gave them joy, but they did not use this wealth to make offerings to the Three Jewels or as alms for the poor. Those people who envied the riches of others also experience these sufferings of hunger and thirst. Those who feel the pain of nakedness are those who did not wear their own clothes but envied the attire of others. And now, even though they possess abundant clothing, food, and riches, they are unable to eat or wear clothes. Even though they have access to as much water as they want—equal to an ocean—they cannot drink; their sufferings of hunger and thirst are inconceivable!"

These beings said to me, "Tell the people on the earth not to show hatred, envy, or greed. They should make strong efforts to engage in good actions, and to help expiate our sins, they should erect a stupa. If they have the yogis perform water offerings for us, we will be liberated from these sufferings. If they do not do these things, we will not be freed for one hundred kalpas."
OM MANI PADME HUM HRIH.

After her visit to the Hell of the Preta, Sangay Choezom assisted in the torture of those who had committed sexual sins, those who sold weapons and used these to kill, and finally those who smoked or chewed tobacco.

I saw an acolyte with the head of an owl and a blue body, dressed in a tiger skin and a green sash, leading the dead bound at the waist with a black rope he held in his hand. He then crushed all sorts of people under a great *vajra* mountain which was as high as eighteen mountains one on top of the other. A large fire burned inside the heads of some; a large *vajra* was planted in the hearts of others.

Some were bound at their feet with rope. Others were crushed by a great *vajra* with their face against the earth. After having seen such sufferings, I asked what was happening, and the god replied to me as follows: "*OM MANI PADME HUM HRIH*. Alas, my daughter, listen well. This place where people are crushed under a great mountain is called Vajra Hell. The acolyte with the head of an owl is the guardian of the entrance to this Vajra Hell. Those who suffer, crushed under the mountain, were once lamas and ordained monks who followed monastic rules, but they broke their vows and wandered the countryside. This is why they experience such retribution and have fallen into the Vajra Hell. Those whose heads burn with large flames broke rules and disobeyed when they were disciples; those who have molten red copper poured into their mouths are experiencing this punishment for having drunk beer when practicing dharma; the ones who have a *vajra* embedded in their heart broke their secret vows; those with chained feet are experiencing this retribution for having engaged in business while practicing dharma; those being crushed flat are experiencing this retribution for having squandered what belonged to the sangha; those experiencing the punishment of the Vajra Hell broke their vows—acts for which they will not be delivered.

I saw in this place a heap of religious books piled high like a mountain, beneath which were innumerable dead. I also saw incalculable numbers of people crushed beneath a stupa, under a house as large as a mountain, and under a great rock. Innumerable people were crushed between two stones. Others carried a rock as large as a mountain on their backs. Many had a ritual dagger (*phurba*) embedded in their bodies. I also saw animals trampling the bodies of men. I saw an acolyte with the head of a deer seize the sinners around the waist with a chain and lead them onward. I saw an acolyte with the head of an elephant take in his hand a great stone and press it down on the hearts of people. I saw an acolyte with the head of a bear take a saw and cut the bodies of the dead into little pieces.

As I watched such unimaginable sufferings, I asked the yidam, and he replied, "*OM MANI PADME HUM HRIH*. Alas, my daughter, listen well. Those crushed under the religious books are experiencing this retribution for having, when on earth, skipped passages in reciting the texts too quickly—now they suffer by being crushed. Those smashed under the stupa are experiencing this for having taken sacred mantras from stupas. Those people crushed under the weight of the house said wicked things and failed to give shelter to travelers when living in the human realm. Those crushed under the great rock are those who worked with stone; they are experiencing this retribution for having killed the little creatures that live among the stones. Those crushed between the two rocks are experiencing this retribution for having killed their fleas. Those who carry rocks made horses and mules carry huge burdens. Those who have a magical dagger (*phurba*) embedded in their bodies are experiencing this for having practiced black magic. Those trampled by animals are experiencing this for having killed all sorts of animals, and they must pay for those deaths. The different people bound by a rope are experiencing this for having killed many wild animals; the deer-headed acolyte will take them into the House of Iron Hell. The beings who practiced destructive rituals to cause harm to others must face the punishment of the elephant-headed acolyte leaning on their hearts with a giant rock. The men whose bodies are cut into pieces by the acolyte with the head of a bear experience this retribution for having killed little creatures when cutting wood. Those whose heads are pushed by a large tree are experiencing this for having taken their own lives by water or by fire. Those who endure the sufferings caused by their actions are inconceivable in number. They suffer in the bardo based on what they did when they were in the land of human beings.

OM MANI PADME HUM HRIH.

We then arrived at a vast plain. There were acolytes—numbering some thirty thousand—with the heads of tigers, bulls, garudas, monkeys, and pigs. They were dressed in tiger skins and whole human skins, wearing bone ornaments and sashes. Their bodies were different colors; they had three eyes and fierce expressions. They carried weapons and appeared to be dancing. About half of them occupied the upper part of the plain and the other half the lower part. In this place the dead were more numerous than the grains of sand in the world or stars in the sky. Their number was beyond imagination. Some cried, naked, their faces turned in the direction of their home country; others cried looking toward paradise; others wept on seeing the acolytes. I saw vast numbers of people: some were happy looking toward the human realm; others prostrated themselves in the direction of paradise; others again were happy and profited from wealth and food. There were those who carried religious texts on their backs. Others held on to prayer flags with the six-syllable mantra. There were innumerable people, both bound and free, and they seem to no longer fear the acolytes.

I asked my yidam, "I see all sorts of people. Some are happy, others weep and lament, others are thirsty and on fire. How can this be?"

The yidam replied, "*OM MANI PADME HUM HRIH*. Alas, my daughter, listen well! This great plain of a kalpa is also called the Land of the Great Bardo of Existence. It is also called the Great City of Hells of Rebirth. Innumerable acolytes are assembled here. The tenth, fifteenth, and thirtieth days of the month are days of fasting for the Eighteen Hells. On those days the acolytes all assemble here. Those in the upper part of the plain are the masters of the hot hells, site of the Great Cauldron. Those on the lower part of the plain are the masters of the cold hells, where the Great Lake is found. On these three auspicious days, they liberate the dead; they do not torment them, and the dead are delivered from the hells. They arrive at the Plain of Rebirth. Those who have undergone a bad rebirth in the eighteen realms come to this Plain of Rebirth during these three days. Those who weep, naked, with their faces turned to the heavens experience this retribution for the sin of killing when in the human realm. Those who weep with their chest flat on the ground experience this retribution for having broken monastic discipline. When they come to the Plain of Rebirth from the Vajra Hell, they repent, and tears flow from their eyes. Those who weep looking in the direction of the human realms are those who have been delivered from the Great Cauldron; they are hoping that good actions will be made for them on the earth, and they suffer from nostalgia as they look toward their lands. Those who weep and look in the direction of paradise repent and weep because the kalpa that will allow them to be delivered has not yet arrived. Those who weep looking at the path to the land of humans hope that the excellent lamas will come in search of sinners like themselves. Those who weep looking at the acolytes meet this retribution for having mistreated other human beings when they were alive on the earth; they repent and weep. The beings of the eight cold hells and the eight hot hells come to the Plain of Rebirth during these three auspicious days. Each day they die one hundred times and are reborn one hundred times.

Those who rejoice looking at the land of humans, they say, will depart once they have been liberated from here. Those who prostrate with faith in the direction of paradise will go to the pure lands once they have been delivered from the impure wheel of rebirth. Those who profited from various riches and foods have acquired merit from making offerings and donations; they collect the fruit of the merit created in the bardo and they are happy. Those who carried holy texts on their backs with the intention that people read religious books obtain the benefits right here in the Plain of Rebirth.

Those who hold a prayer flag with the six-syllable mantra receive the benefit of having erected many prayer flags, and when they are in the bardo, they are happy. The acolytes who come here have a peaceful appearance. Among the innumerable dead, some will return to the hells as before, and some will go to the six destinies. There are those who will return to the land of people, and there are even those who will go to paradise. The other beings who are happy return to their respective lands. The frontier between those who ascend and those who descend is here on the Great Plain of the Hells of Rebirth.

OM MANI PADME HUM HRIH.

Sangay Choezom and her yidam then visited the Hell of Black Lines, where those who have committed the crimes of making war, committing atrocities against humans and animals, and profaning sacred sites suffer. They arrive in front of four houses surrounded by black smoke. Outside, the butchers, arsonists, thieves, swindlers, and finally those who broke their agreements are being tortured. Inside, hunters, the impious, tobacco smokers, the wasteful, and smugglers of precious materials are tortured. Sangay Choezom receives messages from two of them.

Finally, arriving at the Plain of Rebirth, a man dressed in white appeared and said to me, "You, my daughter, how did you come here to the bardo? Do you not recognize me? I will introduce myself—I am your maternal uncle, Tsering Paljor. When in the human realm I was a vagrant; I wandered the world and committed many bad deeds. In the beginning, my retribution was to carry a heavy load, after which I spent three years in the Great Cauldron. Since today is an auspicious day, I have come here. I have endured the numerous sufferings of hunger and thirst; my daughter, give me something to eat!"

"Alas, listen my uncle! The people in the bardo who must endure the sufferings of the hot and cold hells and who suffer from hunger and thirst, what have they done to deserve these punishments? When I left the earth, the Lord of the Dead ordered me to make a tour of the towns of the Eighteen Hells and to be the messenger between the living and the dead, because there is a prediction that I will return to the human realm. What must be done to purify your sins, my uncle?" I offered him a piece of food from the human realm, and my uncle seized the food and said to me, "Because you will return to the human realm, tell my niece and my nephews, my brothers, my children, and my whole family that in order to obtain my deliverance from the bardo, they must read the *Narak dong sprugs*, which is the text for purification of sins. They must copy the *Vajracchedika* text one thousand times, raise prayer flags inscribed with the six syllables, and have the yogis perform the water offering ritual. If you do these good actions, I will obtain rebirth in the human realm."

But he had no chance to eat the food that I had given him because a great red wind carried him away. A storm came across the Plain of Rebirth, and my uncle was carried off before me by the red whirlwind. Abundant tears ran from my eyes and I fainted. The yidam seized my right shoulder and said to me, "*OM MANI PADME HUM HRIH*. Hey, my daughter, get up! Daughter of a good family, listen well. As he endures this suffering due to the weight of his own actions, you can do nothing about the destiny of your sinner uncle. But he has now arrived in the Plain of Rebirth and the acolytes no longer frighten him, and on seeing you, he was delivered. Don't suffer anymore and get up."

OM MANI PADME HUM HRIH.

Then there appeared a man wearing yellow robes like those of a lama turning a prayer wheel. He recited the Mani mantra, and I saw him go toward the Great Cauldron of Hell. He went around the outside of the great dark red cauldron three times, grabbed the edge of the cauldron, and turned it upside down. He then climbed a staircase of five steps—white like conch shells—to the top of the cauldron and said the following words.

"*OM MANI PADME HUM HRIH*. If the dead of the Eighteen Hells below do not recognize me, I will introduce myself. I come from the region of Kham Ling Palri in eastern Tibet. My name is Lama Pema Namgyal, and I have come here from earth to lead all of the dead to paradise. The sinners who did not accumulate good deeds but only bad ones, those who have endured the innumerable sufferings of the hot and cold hells, I will lead them to the marvelous Paradise of Mount Potala. Those who have a bond with me from offering food, they will go up! Those who are inside the Great Cauldron, those who have committed the sin of numerous killings, I will lead them to the marvelous Paradise of Guru Rinpoche. Those who have a religious bond with me, they will go up! Those whose skin is taken from their bodies in the towns of hell, I will lead them to the Paradise of Kubera. Those who have a physical connection with me, they will go up and I will lead them to the Western Paradise. Those who disobeyed their parents and their lamas, those who suffered in the Hell of Black Lines, and those who suffered anger in their spirits, they will go up! I will lead them to the marvelous Paradise of Akanistha. Those who committed the sins of avarice and jealousy—suffering in the Hell of Hungry and Thirsty Beings—if they abandon their avarice, they will go up! I will lead them to the Paradise of Tushita. Those who endure the sufferings of the Hell of Lamentation and Tears, if they abandon their pride, they will go up! I will lead them to the Paradise of the excellent Buddha Aksobhya. Those who carry on their backs their retribution enclosed in the Iron Mountain and have abandoned their attachment to material goods, they will go up!

I am Lama Pema Namgyal. By leaving the obligations of the world behind me, I practice the holy dharma for the benefit of my future life. I recite the Mani mantra for the welfare of all beings of the six destinies. I am a man who has given up attachment. Those who have a bond with me, they will go up!"

I then saw almost three hundred thousand people, delivered from their sufferings, follow the lama on the white road leading to paradise.

OM MANI PADME HUM HRIH.

A voice—not from one of the corpses—rang out from space, and we heard these words clearly: "You two, have you seen the sufferings of the Eighteen Hells? Now, come and see the Lord of the Dead." As the yidam and I prepared to climb there, we arrived at the palace of the Lord of the Dead. He appeared in the same form as before, and I saw the god and the demon separating white actions from black actions. I saw the acolytes behave in the same terrifying way as the first time. Innumerable dead arrived at this place. The acolyte with the head of a bull seized one of the dead with a cord and took him before the Lord of the Dead, who said to him, "Hey, you dead person, listen! After your death, you arrived here in the bardo. From which region of the earth are you from? Tell me your name and the status of your family. Which black sins did you commit?

Which good, white actions did you perform? Confess frankly all of the good and bad actions, because if you do not confess fully now, here on this field I will cut you up with my sword!"

I saw that the Lord of the Dead, after speaking, looked at the dead person with his three flaming eyes. Abundant tears flowed from the eyes of the man, who said, "*OM MANI PADME HUM HRIH*. Alas, Lord of the Dead, listen to this deceased man who asks for your attention! I am from the earth, the Continent of the South. The name of my land is Kurtoe, and I am called Tandin Phuntsho. When I was in the land of the living, I had to commit many sins in order to obtain food and clothing. I killed twenty pigs to nourish myself. I also killed many birds, boars, goats, and sheep. I blasphemed against the lamas who lived in the high valley. I abused my position of power over the villagers. When seven foreign merchants arrived in the country, I robbed them to feed my children, and I committed innumerable other sins. I do not remember the sins that I committed in the second half of my life. When a manipa came to my land, the people recited the Mani mantra, and I went to recite Mani as well. This manipa described at length the terrors of the bardo, the sins, and the good actions from the biography of the delom Lingza Chokyi. And there was born in my spirit a deep regret for my sins, and I asked myself what I could do to atone for them. I made offerings and gave services to the manipa to create a bond between us, and I gave several services to members of the sangha. I offered food to yogis who came begging. These are my good actions, though I arrived here after having committed a great number of bad black actions. I am not protected by the Three Jewels. I do not have the support of the dakinis and protectors. I have not gained merit for having recited the Mani mantra. Do not send me below into the Eighteen Hells, great Lord of the Dead, but be compassionate toward me!" And he repeated, "Alas!" and I saw him prostrate three times.

The black demon to his right stood up and said, "Ha, ha! I have a few things to say to you, Lord of the Dead. This sinner, whose name was Tandin Phuntsho when he was alive, blasphemed against the lamas and members of the sangha. He showed himself to be an ingrate toward the kindness of his parents, he stole from merchants, and he mistreated his children. He abused his power by taking what had not been given to him. He killed many sheep, goats, boars, and birds." Addressing the man, he said, "You say that you engaged in good actions—that is a lie! There is no other place in which to punish you than in these hells! Here, more or less, counted in pebbles are all of the wicked actions that you committed." And he filled up three measures of black pebbles.

The white god to his left side stood up. "Great Lord of the Dead, hear me! He gave service to lamas and to members of the sangha. He gave food to the manipas to create a bond with them. He was a friend of the villagers. Here are the pebbles which show his accumulated virtue." And he filled three measures of white pebbles.

Then the acolyte with the head of a monkey said, "As the god and the demon do not agree, I will weigh the black and white pebbles on my scales." The white pebbles placed on the scales were lighter than the black pebbles. Then the acolyte with the head of a serpent looked into the Mirror of Deeds. The good deeds numbered fewer than the black misdeeds.

The Lord of the Dead then said, "Your two speeches, god and demon, are half true and half false." And he addressed the following words to the man, "When you were alive, you obtained a human body, very precious, but you did not accomplish a single religious act that will benefit you. You accumulated innumerable bad actions. You have more bad deeds than good deeds. There is no other place to punish you than the hells. The punishment for having killed twenty animals is to spend fifty years in the Great Cauldron. The punishment for having blasphemed against the lamas is to stay in the Vajra Hell for eighty years. The punishment for having taken what was not given to you is to be pinned under a great rock for one thousand years. The punishment for greed and anger is to go to the Hell of Lamentation and Tears and and the Hell of Hungry and Thirsty Beings. The punishment for having abused your power over people is to be stuck in the Hell of Black Lines for one hundred years. The punishment for having mistreated your children is to spend ninety years in Shalmali. The punishment for having disobeyed your parents is to live beneath a great rock for one thousand years. The punishment for greed and anger is to remain under a mountain for one hundred thousand years."

"Those who steal from other men become interested in giving service to lamas and the sangha to purify their sins after having stolen. Those who commit the wicked actions of killing animals such as pigs and birds are interested in giving service to manipas and reciting the Mani mantra to purify their sins after having performed the terrible deeds. The punishment for this wickedness and covetousness is to be reborn in the Hell of Unceasing Tortures and to be delivered only after a kalpa has passed. As a result of your innumerable sins, the moment has arrived to go to the hell realms. People may cry and wail but all to no avail at this moment."

After the Lord of the Dead had spoken, he called three times for the acolyte with the head of a bull and ordered him to bind this sinner with his cord and lead him to the hell realms. The acolyte rose up and laughed three times, "Ha, Ha, Ha!" and I saw him bind the man around his waist and lead him to the hell realms. I saw other acolytes beat the man with black axes, others pierced his back with swords, while others seized his feet and took him away. The acolytes uttered terrifying cries of "*Hum, hum, phat, phat!*"

The yidam said, "You, acolytes, hear me! Do you utter such terrifying cries because of the sins committed by this man? Here is someone who will go back to the land of the living. Certainly, this man has committed sins but there are ways to atone for them. Loosen him a little from his bonds and allow him to give a message to the world of the living."

The acolytes replied, "You, divine daughter, listen to us! We acolytes do not abuse our power. The time has come for this dead person to go to the hell realms because of his accumulated actions." They loosened his bonds a little, and this man gave me the following message. "Alas, alas, as you are from the earth, daughter of good karma, carry this message from the sinner that I am. I was born in

Kurtoe. My wife is called Pedan Drolma. Out of compassion for me, please have my son, my daughter, and my whole family send me merit. Have them recite the *Contrition of Sins* to purify my actions for having killed twenty animals. Have them copy the text *One Hundred Thousand Verses of the Buddha* and also copy the *Hundred Names of the Divinities of the Bardo* to purify the sins of having blasphemed against lamas. They should erect a standard of prayer flags with the six-syllable mantra, and they should perform water offerings for the hungry and thirsty beings to purify the sins of greediness and the abuse of power. They should have a statue of Buddha Aksobhya made so that I may be delivered from the Hell of Unceasing Tortures. They should give services and make offerings to the manipas so that I may be delivered from the sufferings of the Eighteen Hells. For three weeks, they should recite the Mani mantra and offer food and drink to the villagers. When they have accomplished these good actions, I will be delivered from the hells and I will obtain a rebirth in the Continent of the West. Tell everybody well-versed in the ways of the world that such deeds are like nothing when one reaches the bardo. Give this message to the whole world." The acolytes bound him and carried him away as before.

OM MANI PADME HUM HRIH.

A man arrived below from the land of humans. He wore a red and yellow robe, his hair was pulled into a ponytail, and he carried prayer beads in his hand; he carried a statue on his back and muttered a prayer. The man walked around the Lord of the Dead three times, prostrated three times, and then stood in front of him. The Lord of the Dead posed the same questions to him as to the previous man, and this man replied, "Alas, hear me, Lord of the Dead. I am a mendicant who has abandoned bad actions. I am from Paro in western Bhutan, of the lineage of Pema, and my name is Ngawang Paljor. I left all obligations of the world, and I abandoned negative actions. I am abstinent. As I thought of the terrors that awaited me in the bardo, I sought the teachings of many lamas. Without attachment to riches, clothes, or food, I retired alone to the mountains, and there I practiced dharma. I circumambulated holy sites and prostrated to purify my carnal sins. To clean the stains of my speech, I recited the six-syllable mantra. To purify the stains of my thoughts, I meditated on the *Cycle of Clear Light*. I recited a million times the Vajra Guru mantra of Padmasambhava. I undertook pilgrimages to the great and small mountains. I stayed in retreat for eleven years at Paro Taktsang, the holy place blessed by Guru Rinpoche. Benefactors gave me food and clothing, and although I did not practice dharma intensely, I did engage a little in the way of the teachings. I have no protector or hope except for you. Do not send me to the hell realms; instead I ask you to send me to the field of deliverance, to the place of paradise."

The black demon who was to his right stood up and said, "This wicked man who is called Ngawang Paljor, when he was small, he killed three beings. He ate enormous amounts of offerings for the living and the dead. He says that he practiced dharma—that is a lie! Here, more or less, is a count of the sins that he accumulated." The demon filled a half-measure of black pebbles.

The white god who was to his left stood up and made his report to the Lord of the Dead. "This yogi called Ngawang Paljor has accomplished a great deal of white actions. He has left behind him the bad actions. Alone, he abandoned the world, and he practiced dharma. He received gifts of food and clothing, and he recited the Mani mantra. To purify his sins of body, speech, and mind, he made many circumambulations and prostrations. He always prayed to Guru Rinpoche and recited a million Vajra Guru mantras. He is not somebody to be sent to the hell realms. This is a man to be sent to the land of the Vidyadharas. Here is the count of the virtuous actions he has accumulated." And he made a huge pile with the white pebbles.

The Lord of the Dead said, "Look into the Mirror of Deeds." He looked into the mirror and smiled. "It is excellent that those who engage in good actions on the earth, in the land of humans, are few in number. The god said that you practiced dharma, and that is true. You, white god, escort this man to the land of the Vidyadharas."

This man gave me his message, "Listen, my daughter of good karma! Take this message to Paro, in the region of the West. My name is Ngawang Paljor. Give this message to my sister, Chodron. When I was in the land of the living, I left behind all my worldly responsibilities. When I came to the bardo, I received the benefit of having exclusively practiced the dharma. I did not have any fear, and I went to the land of the Vidyadharas. You, my sister, for the good of your future life, offer all that you have to the lamas. Food and goods accumulated through greed—give them as offerings to the mendicants. After abandoning the sins of covetousness and maliciousness, constantly recite the six-syllable mantra. Give this message to all sinners: This man was taken away to the land of the Vidyadharas!"

With these words he left for the land of the Vidyadharas.

OM MANI PADME HUM HRIH.

Sangay Choezom visits two regions of paradise and gives a detailed description. In one, she views the palaces of the Buddhas and Bodhisattvas, Vajrasattva, Ratnasambhava, Nangwa Thaye, Amogasiddhi, Mahakaruna, Karsapana, and Arya Mahakaruna. In the other, she visits the palaces of Aksobhya, Guru Rinpoche, Amitabha, and Manjushri. In each paradise, she sees people rejoicing and engaging in religious activities. The yidam explains to her their significance, since these actions lead to rebirth in paradise.

From the side of the bridge below, a yogi said to me, "Daughter, since you died, seven days have passed in the land of human beings. Your parents and your family have started the preparations to cremate your body. Quickly, return there!"

I thought that I should return, so I came into the presence of the Lord of the Dead. A daughter of mankind, dressed in red, was also in front of the Lord of the Dead, and he spoke to her thus, "Hey, my daughter, listen well! You have almost passed seven human lives. In this birth you must be a messenger between the living and the dead." And she replied to him thus, "Lord of the Dead, please listen to me. In accordance with your orders, I have visited completely the three states of the bardo. When I returned to the land of human beings, my body had already been burned. I was not able to deliver the message, and I had to return here to your presence. Lord of the Dead, I request permission to take another birth." The Lord of the Dead then said, "*OM MANI PADME HUM HRIH*. Hey, my daughter, listen carefully to my words! For this birth, you will be reborn on the edge of China. You will be reborn as the son of wealthy people, but when you attain the age of eighteen, you will return here, and you will be a messenger between the living and the dead as before. The place for your activities—for the benefit of these beings—is on the edge of China. *OM MANI PADME HUM HRIH*."

This girl said to me, "As they say that you will return to the land of human beings, daughter of good family, take my message. I was born near Tawang on the south side of the Himalayas, the name of my village is Tsang Podrong and I am called Dorje Lhamo. When I arrived at the land of the bardo, I met the Lord of the Dead and made a seven-day tour of the bardo. When I returned to the land of human beings, my corpse had already been burned and had disappeared. As I had not received this prophecy before, I was not able to be reunited with my family, my brothers and sisters, and my parents. I have not been subject to the tortures of hell, but I have obtained a rebirth in the land of human beings on the edge of China." With these words she left upward, following a yellow path. *OM MANI PADME HUM HRIH*.

Then, from the other side of the bridge, a gomchen dressed in red called out to us: "You two, if you do not return to the land of human beings above, the corpse of this girl will soon be burned!" With that, the man flew off toward the west. My divine yidam made numerous circumambulations of the Lord of the Dead, prostrated himself toward his feet, and then said, "Lord of the Dead, please hear what I have to say. Since we arrived, seven days in human time have elapsed. The parents of this girl will prepare her corpse, her material body. According to a previous prophecy, she must bring messages to the land of human beings, is that not correct? Are you going to send her to the paradise above, or are you going to send her to one of the six destinies? I ask that you now decide where to send this girl."

The Lord of the Dead looked at Sangey Choezom with a terrifying gaze, then he entered into meditation. Some moments later his large eyes opened, and he looked into the Mirror of Deeds. He then uttered these words, "You have been born eleven times on earth without mistaken name or lineage. Without knowing the year, you arrived in my presence on the thirtieth day of the sixth month of the Fire Dog Year. Have you seen the places where sins and good actions are accounted for? Have you also seen the terrors inflicted by the acolytes? Have you visited the paradises of the Buddhas? Have you understood that I am the Lord of the Dead? As in the past, you were again reborn as a human being, you venerated Arya Avalokiteshvara, and you practiced dharma perfectly. This is why you are experiencing this blessing now, and why you must be a messenger between the living and the dead. The lords of your land say that your body of flesh and blood is the incarnation of a demon, and they have bound your hands and feet. Your parents suffer. When you arrive back on earth, you will hear different people say wicked words. Some will say that you are a demon, others that you are lying, while others will say that you are the incarnation of Buddha. Many will say that they are not certain exactly what you are or are not. At that moment, a being will obtain realization, an incarnation of the Buddha will arrive from the south and will say to you, 'My daughter, you are the incarnation of Avalokiteshvara Mahakaruna; it is you who is the messenger between the living and the dead. My daughter, you must explain to them in detail the stories of the bardo of human beings and hide nothing from them. You will accomplish benefits for all beings.' Then two monks will appear from the north and say to you, 'My daughter, go into the presence of your lama—Ngawang Samten—and after you arrive, he will ask you questions concerning the terrors of the bardo. You must explain to him the stories of the Eighteen Hells.' Such is the prophecy from your previous lives, and this is your karma. From these actions, beings will receive great benefit."

So said the Lord of the Dead, and he added, "My daughter, listen to me well. Pass on the messages from here to those on earth. Tell all the people on earth that these are the words of the Lord of the Dead: OM MANI PADME HUM HRIH. Those who are born on earth in the Continent of the South, when they obtain a precious human body, refrain from accumulating the hellish seeds of sins! Rather, they must abandon the sin of killing and engage in good actions! They should meditate on the doctrine of the Mahamudra! They should not consciously commit sins, and they must not kill wild animals or birds. Tell them of the dangers of falling into the Hell of the Great Cauldron. They should not be proud, angry, or jealous! Otherwise, these traits will send them to the hot hells! They should not steal the clothes of others, or this will send them to the cold hells! They should not commit any action that requires the preparation of poison, or they will be cooked in the Lake of Black Poison! They should not tell lies or slander, or their tongues will be pulled out by iron pincers. They must not disobey their kind parents, or they will be crushed under the three worlds! They should not feel avarice for the riches that they accumulate, or they will endure the sufferings of hunger and thirst! When reciting holy books they should not skip passages, or they will be crushed under a large mountain! They must not be rough toward the little people (the poor) or they will fall into the Hell of Lamentation and Tears! Even if they keep their religious vows and discipline, they should not develop an attachment for women, or they will be placed in the Iron Hell of Shalmali! They should not be grasping or wicked, or thousands of nails will be hammered into their bodies! They must never kill the children that they give birth to, or they will be sent to hell with no hope of liberation!"

"Women should not seek to seduce the husbands of others, or boiling bronze liquid will be poured into their vaginas. All monks should keep monastic discipline, or they will be placed in the Vajra Hell. They should not pretend to save the dead when they themselves are not accomplished, or they will be thrown into the Lake of Blood!"

"People who sell goods should not fix or cheat with their weights and measures, or their bodies will be cut into small pieces and used as weights on the scales. They should not appropriate riches not given to them by their parents, or they will fall into the place of lamentations where beings are hungry and thirsty! They should not commit blasphemy or other forms of impiety toward the meditators of both sexes who have retreated to the mountains, nor toward the manipas who wander the country, or they will be placed in the Iron House with No Door. They should not kill innocent people, or they will be placed in the Iron Mountain and crushed under religious texts. They should not betray the confidence of others, or their bodies will be boiled and placed in their mouths. They should not practice black magic or nefarious incantations! They should not kill animals that they themselves have reared, or they themselves will be carved up. They should not shear or harm animals, or they will be placed in the Hell of Black Lines. They should not cheat when selling meat but be honest, or they will be crushed under a large rock. They should not steal from houses or commit theft, or they will be tortured by being cut into small pieces! They should not mistreat other human beings or abuse their power, or they will be beaten around the head with a black hammer! They should not set fire to the mountain forests, or they will be tortured by being burned on a great bonfire. They should not remove the sacred mantras and formulas from inside statues or stupas—for these are the Body and Mind support of the Buddha—or they will be crushed under a great stupa. They should not kill themselves, or they will die one hundred times each day on the Plain of Rebirth. They should not sell beer to lamas or members of the sangha, or they will be crushed under a great mountain! They should not engage in warfare or commit crimes, or they will be sent to the Hell of Unceasing Torments."

The Lord of the Dead, living far below, distinctly separates the white good actions from the black bad actions. Sinners who have committed sins in relation to tobacco are not sent to the Hell of Black Lines, but rather to the Eighteen Hells! Those people who have white good actions are sent to the fields of deliverance!

"If all people on the earth followed my commands, I would appear to them not as the Lord of the Dead, but in fact as Avalokiteshvara, the Great Compassionate One! They should recite the six-syllable mantra, the essential mantra! I may have the appearance of the Lord of the Dead, but in fact I am Guru Rinpoche! They should recite the mantra, *VAJRA GURU SIDDHI*! All people should repent their past negative acts! They should avoid committing negative actions in the future, or they will be subject to the innumerable tortures of the hot and cold hells! The road to the land of the bardo is long, and sinners should repent their faults. Without refuge or protection they wail and weep. They should remember that their lama is always with them at the top of their head! Without being separated from their deity, they should meditate with him at their heart. After making offerings of butter lamps and incense at the temples where there are statues and books—supports of the Body and Speech of the Buddha—they should make numerous circumambulations and prostrations! While they are able to, they should practice the dharma! They should donate the riches they have gathered through avarice! Here is the message of the Lord of the Dead: Present this to all those who live on the earth."

OM MANI PADME HUM HRIH.

And the Lord of the Dead again declared, "You, my child, when you go on pilgrimage to the large and small mountains and visit the places where in the past delog Karma Wangzin lived, all the people will come to interrogate you at length about your experiences in the bardo. Among them will be those predestined to hell, and you must explain what you have seen in the bardo without hiding anything. You must encourage people to practice the dharma. Your lama will speak to you in the same way as me. You must go to the fortress of Punakha, seat of the Bhutanese government. Among the lords and people, young and old, certain among them will venerate you and have faith in you; others will slander you and throw impious glances toward you. There will be those who say different things. You must give them explanations without hesitation, and from your actions will come great benefit for all beings. During the course of your life you will experience difficulties; you will have a problem when you are thirty; but at that moment, the date of your death will be pushed back, and you will return here when you are fifty. Despite your fear of the acolytes, we will meet again like a father and his child. Then you will be reborn in the world, in a hidden and blessed land (*beyul*). There you will be called Dechen Wangmo. Once you have finished converting the people there, you will be reborn in the land of Oddiyana, land of the dakinis. Do not eat fish, pork, or eggs! Your mind understands perfectly my words! Above, they are preparing to cremate your body, so you must now return to the earth."

The dead then cried out, "Alas, as he said that you are to go to the land of the living, daughter of good family, say this to all those living in the land of men: 'That they should cease to commit the sin of killing, that they should make every effort to do good white actions, and that they should recite continuously the six-syllable mantra! Thus, when they attain the bardo, nothing but good will come to them." And the innumerable dead watched me leave.

OM MANI PADME HUM HRIH.

As I was thinking that I should go back up, a green wind blew and carried me upward. In an instant, I arrived at Zachu Gang, my village. I encountered a woman who had come in search of water, and we walked together. I did not recognize my body, and I saw that it looked like the body of a pig. As I said to myself that I did not know what it was, I lost consciousness. My body then moved a little, and a man who was there checked to see whether or not there was any warmth in my heart. Yes, there was a little warmth in my heart. The seven women who were watching over my body cried out, "The girl has returned!" and they began to cry and shout. My mother then arrived and raised the cloth. Crying to herself—"My daughter, have you come back?"—she took my hand and began to cry and shout. At dawn on the seventh day my entire village exclaimed, "The girl has returned from the Land of the Dead!" They came to see me and talked a great deal. My parents and family offered me various things to drink. But since my soul and my body had been separated for seven days, my throat was so dry that I was unable to drink even water. The pious men there asked me where I had gone for seven days, and many women of faith looked at me and wept. Other ordinary people were jealous and angry. Those beings with good karma made prostrations and circumambulations. Numerous sinners were incredulous, and these demons said to me that I was not telling the truth. All the people gathered around me and earnestly requested that I recount what had passed during my time in the bardo.

OM MANI PADME HUM HRIH.

I then gave them this report. "I abandoned the human realm for seven days. I left in the company of my divine yidam, and I arrived in the presence of the Lord of the Dead, who said to me these words precisely. 'You must visit the Eighteen Hells. You must visit all of the realms of paradise. You must be the messenger between the living and the dead.' This message from the Lord of the Dead is more precious than gold, this very precious jewel. All those on earth should refrain from black sins! As for all the riches and foodstuffs accumulated through greed, these should be offered to the Three Jewels and be given as alms to the poor! All people should be encouraged to practice dharma! Today, I have returned from the Lord of the Dead after seven days!"

OM MANI PADME HUM HRIH.

Here is the story of the journey to the Eighteen Hells by the revenant Sangay Choezom, including the message of the Lord of the Dead and messages from the dead in the Other World.

OM MANI PADME HUM HRIH. SARVA MANGALAM.

Wamrong Delog.

AFTERWORD

FRANÇOISE POMMARET

In this book, we concentrated on exploring the lives of the divine messengers from western Bhutan. Although the situation of these women is slightly different in other parts of Bhutan, it generally follows the same pattern. For example, in the Tang valley of Bumthang, one elderly pamo (called *nyenjom* in western Bhutan) who no longer practices due to her ill health insisted that she cannot pass her powers to a member of her family or anyone else, because it is not up to her to decide who should succeed her; that is the decision of the deity. If the deity does not manifest in somebody, then there will be no pamo.

Kunzang Choden wrote about this issue in an autobiographical short story, "The Woman Who Lost her Senses" in her book, *Tales in Color.* Also located in the Tang valley, this story recounts the tragic life of a villager who lost her senses because "the deities choose the mediums. Mediums do not get to choose their deities. My mother's deities were powerful, and it is their anger that makes me like this."

It seems that the villager's mother was a pamo who was violently beaten and subjugated by a Tibetan Buddhist lama who came to the village in the mid-twentieth century; he was against this manifestation of what he believed was an evil Bon belief. Her mother was a broken person after that, and her deity, who was from Tibet, never appeared again. She died soon thereafter. A deity from Haa (probably Ap Chundu) then manifested in her elder sister, who became a pamo as well. But her sister did not try to teach her, because their mother's deity should have possessed her—yet never did.

This story illustrates the complex and intimate relationship between local deities and Buddhist deities, and their mediums, which the old pamo in Tang also puts in simple words: "Now I am too old to perform, and because of that, sometimes my deity comes and cries in me. Unless the deity chooses somebody else after I die, there will be no pamo for this deity."

The divine messengers depend totally on their deities; they were chosen by them and are their voices. They are not free to make decisions regarding their role without praying to them. In eastern Bhutan, a delom whom I met in 2014 in a village opposite Trashigang told me, "I was chosen to be a delom by Avalokiteshvara, but I was too afraid to be cremated before I came back from the hells. So I requested Avalokiteshvara to relieve me, and to make up for my shortcoming, I spend a lot of time in meditation in sacred places and pray for the sentient beings."

This is a world where humans and deities are not separated, but it is also a world that has had to resist attempts to be broken either by certain purist Buddhist lamas or by the state, which had also attempted at times to suppress these nonorthodox religious believers. Their position is linked to the local deities who are considered on a low rung of the Buddhist pantheon, as they are not enlightened, and they show respect to members of the clergy whom they recognize as being on a higher plane than them. They did not choose to become messengers. This role was imposed on them by external forces. But by saying that they benefit all sentient beings, they express it in a Buddhist way and perform what they see as their duties with a sense of pride.

The divine messengers—or whatever terms they use for themselves or others refer to them as—are an amazing phenomenon that has survived for centuries on the margins of the official religious establishments. From the corpus of delom biographies, of which Sangay Choezom's is an excellent example, to the stories of contemporary practitioners with all their complexities and too-human reactions, the divine messengers fill a socioreligious need in a specific Himalayan society. They address the immediate need and the mundane preoccupations of the ordinary people. Settled in the villages and also from farming families, they belong to the same environment as those they serve and speak with in simple words about daily issues. These women are empowered with a special mission in their own society and are aware of that. They are spiritual healers who alleviate the immediate sufferings of the people and advise them in their conduct, but they operate in a completely different way and on a different plane than the clergy.

Although all present the same pattern of shamanic traits (illness, fainting, a supernatural being ordering them to help people, diet, etc.), they are part of Vajrayana Buddhism, which embraced non-Buddhist characters and allowed them to operate inside that religious framework. This was facilitated by two important aspects of Vajrayana. On one hand, the conversion of local pre-Buddhist deities, a main trope in this form of Buddhism, allowed their human representatives to exist within the Buddhist framework. On the other hand, in Vajrayana the importance of the feminine, which represents wisdom, help on the path of enlightenment, and glorification of female deities, promotes worship of enlightened religious women. The divine messengers we encountered, as simple as they seem, continue to reflect the enduring value of feminine spiritual authority in the Himalayas.

Acknowledgments

We would like to express our heartfelt appreciation and deepest respect to all the divine messengers who have opened up their world to us, patiently demonstrating and explaining their way of life, which they have done freely, for the benefit of all beings. Gratitude to Samten Karmay for his willingness to share his breadth of knowledge, and to Richard Whitecross for his painstakingly detailed translation from French to English of Sangay Choezom's biography. Profound thanks are also due to Chencho Dorji. He has been an endlessly kind and empathic guide, translator, and collaborator. Many thanks to Casey Kemp at Shambhala for her dedication to the big ideas behind this book. Because of her vision, you now hold it in your hands. And our utmost appreciation for the editors and designers at Shambhala who have worked with our manuscript with great sensitivity and care.

My humble gratitude to my dear friend and coauthor, Françoise Pommaret, for her endless patience with my endless questions and her boundless energy and enthusiasm for collaborating with me on this book in all ways. I would not have contemplated undertaking this book without the support of the Shelly and Donald Rubin Foundation, and former Executive Director Alex Gardner in particular, who cheered me along the whole way, as I wound deeper down the path of understanding Vajrayana Buddhism, Bhutan, and the Himalayan world. My dear friend Terry Causey has always grasped the larger vision of my work, reminding me of what I am doing, and has provided the emotional support and financial foundation to be able to pursue this long period of learning and travel and writing. My children, Jasper and Malia, are my moon and stars and my travel companions over many thousands of miles and many years. My husband Dave Worthington has been my solid rock over the years of this writing.

Stephanie Guyer-Stevens

I join my friend Stephanie in thanking the people who were willing to work with us, and I also thank Stephanie for obliging me to come out of my academic comfort zone. My deep gratitude goes to my professors in France, the late Gene E. Smith, who generously helped me as a young researcher, and Mani Dorji from KMT in Thimphu who took me on my first trip in search of the deloms. Of course, I cannot thank enough my friend and great author Kunzang Choden for encouraging me during my endeavors and agreeing to write the foreword.

I would like to thank with my two folded hands the religious teachers I had the good fortune to meet in Bhutan who tried patiently to inculcate in me the notions of compassion and right attitude of the mind. I am a student without much ability, but I hope I did not betray what they taught me.

Françoise Pommaret

NOTES

1. Todd Gibson, "Notes on the History of the Shamanic in Tibet and Inner Asia," *Numen* 44, no. 1 (January, 1997): 39–59. Accessed January 24, 2021, http://www.jstor.org/stable/3270381.
2. Geoffrey Samuel, *Civilized Shamans: Buddhism in Tibetan Buddhist Societies* (Washington and London: Smithsonian Institution Press, 1993), 000.
3. Homayun Sidky, "The State Oracle of Tibet, Spirit Possession, and Shamanism," *Numen* 58, no. 1 (January 2011): 78.
4. Sidky, "The State Oracle of Tibet, Spirit Possession, and Shamanism," 232–33.
5. Sidky, "The State Oracle of Tibet, Spirit Possession, and Shamanism," 71–99.
6. Evans-Wentz, Walter Yelling, and Lama Kazi Dawa-Samdup, eds. *The Tibetan Book of the Dead or The After-Death Experiences on the Bardo Plane* (London: Oxford University Press/Humphrey Milford, 1927). Please note that in the bibliography we have referenced a different translation of the book—the Graham Coleman and Thupten Jinpa version.
7. Anne Marie Blondeau, "Les Religions du Tibet" in *Histoire des religions III* (Paris: Encyclopedie de la Pleiade, 1976), 246–247.
8. http://www.neyphug.org/monastery.html.

Bibliography

Balikci, Anna. *Lamas, Shamans, and Ancestors: Village Religion in Sikkim.* Leiden, Netherlands: Brill, 2008.

Blondeau, Anne-Marie. "Les religions du Tibet." In *Histoire des Religions III.* NRF Encyclopédie de la Pléiade. 233–249. Paris: Gallimard, 1976.

Coleman, Graham, and Thupten Jinpa (eds.). *The Tibetan Book of the Dead,* trans Gyurme Dorje. New York: Penguin Books, 2007.

Cuevas, Bryan J. *Travels in the Netherworld: Buddhist Popular Narratives of Death and the Afterlife in Tibet.* Oxford: Oxford University Press, 2008.

Diemberger, Hildegard. "Female Oracles in Modern Tibet." In *Women in Tibet,* edited by Janet Gyatso and Hanna Havnevik, 113–168. New York: Columbia University Press, 2006.

Epstein, Lawrence. "On the History and Psychology of the Das-Log." *Tibet Journal* 7, no. 4 (1982): 20–85.

Imaeda, Yoshiro. *Histoire du cycle de la naissance et de la mort.* Genève-Paris: Droz, 1981.

Karmay, Samten, and Jeff Watt (eds.). *Bon The Magic Word: The Indigenous Religion of Tibet.* New York: Rubin Museum of Art; London: Philip Wilson Publishers, 2007.

Kumagai, Seiji. *Bhutanese Buddhism and its Culture.* Kathmandu: Vajra Books, 2014.

Lopez Jr., Donald S. (ed.). *Religions of Tibet in Practice.* Princeton, NJ: Princeton University Press, 1997.

Lopez Jr., Donald S. *The Story of Buddhism: A Concise Guide to its History and Teachings.* New York: Harper Collins. 2001.

Peters, Larry. *Tibetan Shamanism and Healing.* Berkeley: North Atlantic Books, 2016.

Phuntsho, Karma. *The History of Bhutan.* India: Random House India, 2015.

Pommaret, Françoise. *Les Revenants de l'Au-delà dans le Monde Tibétain.* Paris: CNRS Éditions, 1989.

———. "Returning from Hell." In *Religions of Tibet in Practice*, edited by Donald Lopez, 499–510. Princeton, NJ: Princeton University Press, 1997.

———. *Tibet: An Enduring Civilization*. New York: Harry N. Abrams, 2003.

———. *Bhutan: Himalayan Mountain Kingdom*. Hong Kong: Odyssey Books, 2007.

Prude, Mary Alyson. "Death, Gender, and Extraordinary Knowing: The Delog ('das log) Tradition in Nepal and Eastern Tibet." PhD dissertation, University of California, Santa Barbara.

———. 2020. "A Reexamination of Marginal Religious Specialists: Himalayan Messengers from the Dead." *Journal of the American Academy of Religion* 88, no. 3 (September 2020): 779–804.

Samuel, Geoffrey. *Civilized Shamans: Buddhism in Tibetan Buddhist Societies*. Washington, D.C.: Smithsonian Institution Press, 1993.

Schneider, Nicola. "Female incarnation lineages: some remarks on their Features and Functions in Tibet." In *From Bhakti to Bon: Festschrift for Per Kvaerne*, edited by H. Havnevik and C. Ramble, 463–479. Oslo, Norway: Novus Forlag, 2015.

Schrempf, Mona, and Nicola Schneider (eds.). "Women as Visionaries, Healers and Agents of Social Transformation in the Himalayas, Tibet and Mongolia." *Revue des Etudes Tibétaines* no. 34 (December 2015).

Sidky, Homayun. "The State Oracle of Tibet, Spirit Possession, and Shamanism." *Numen* 58, no. 1 (January 2011): 71–99.

Snellgrove, David. *The Nine Ways of Bon*. Bangkok: Orchid Press, 2010.

Stein, Rolf. *Tibetan Civilization*. London: Faber and Faber, Ltd., 1972.

STEPHANIE AND FRANÇOISE IN PUNAKHA

ABOUT THE AUTHORS

STEPHANIE GUYER-STEVENS is a writer, community activist, award winning radio producer, and mother. She founded the nonprofit media team Outer Voices to share stories of women and other seldom heard voices.

FRANÇOISE POMMARET is a French anthropologist whose research focuses on Bhutan, where she has worked since 1981 participating in tourism, educational, and cultural projects. She holds the position of director of research at the Centre national de la recherche scientifique (CNRS). Pommaret also works as an associate professor at the College of Language and Cultural Studies (CLCS) at the Royal University of Bhutan, has been a consultant for UNESCO, and is the author of *Bhutan: Himalayan Mountain Kingdom* and *Lhasa in the Seventeenth Century: The Capital of the Dalai Lamas*. She is on the board of several foundations such as Les Amis du Bhoutan in France, the Bhutan Foundation in the United States, and the Loden Foundation in Bhutan.